WHAT READERS

This is the best book I've read on this difficult subject, covering all the major issues of pedophilia in a fascinating human interest way. I am confident this will stand with the best of the literature that is out there. It should be required reading by every ordained person in all denominations—plus lay leaders and others.

—The Rt. Rev. Harold A. Hopkins, DD, Executive Director of the Office of Pastoral Development of the House of Bishops, Episcopal Church, USA (Ret.)

The author tells aloud what happened to him as a child, over sixty years ago, and how that affected him throughout his adult life. Russell's journey is both unique to him, and also a cautionary tale about the abuse of power in the church and other institutions. He writes with the authenticity of one who has overcome what was done to him. In the end, he comes to terms with his own life's story, experiencing the grace that only telling can achieve. I've known Carl Russell for 50 years, and I admire him all the more for telling this truth. Highly recommended!

—The Rev. David P. Illingworth, Associate Dean of Harvard College (Ret.), Episcopal priest, Diocese of Maine

No Telling Aloud

This is a very useful book for individuals . . . a wonderful tool for delving into this thorny issue in small group discussions.

—*Nancy Myer Hopkins, MS, author, consultant to congregations dealing with clergy misconduct*

NO TELLING ALOUD

KEEPING SECRETS
THAT HURT

NO TELLING ALOUD

KEEPING SECRETS
THAT HURT

―――――――

CARL A. RUSSELL, JR.

with

Asa N. Russell

Mill City Press, Minneapolis

FOR MY WIFE
THE REV. MARGARET (GRETA) STREET RUSSELL

TABLE OF CONTENTS

ACKNOWLEDGMENTS — xiii

FOREWORD — xv

INTRODUCTION —*xix*

CHAPTER ONE

THREE DAYS IN MAY – 1954 — 1

Day One – "Don't tell them about us!" — 1

Day Two – Cover-up — 3

Day Three – Liar, liar — 11

CHAPTER TWO

BACKSTORY 1944 –1954 — 17

'Tis the Gift To Be Simple — 17

Migration — 23

In the Beauty of Holiness — 26

The Opera He Never Sang — 30

Mirror, Mirror — 33

The Newly Minted Key — 37

The House with the Funny Name — 41

Shrine — 44

What Are We Doing Here? — 46

Helping Out — 59

The Shadow Knows — 63

I Will Always Be . . . — 66

No Telling Aloud

The Pact — 68
Tower Watch — 74
Camp Is Very Entertaining — 76
After the Ball — 81
Mr. God — 86
Look Around You — 88
Body Language — 89
Good Grooming — 91
Something More — 95

CHAPTER THREE
MOVING ON 1954–1961 — 101
Close Encounter — 101
Take Thou Authority — 104

CHAPTER FOUR
THINGS SEEN AND UNSEEN 1961–1984 — 109
The Invisible Dog — 109
For the Bible Tells Me So. Really? — 115
Friends In High Places — 121

CHAPTER FIVE
FROM THE DEEP 1984–2008 — 127
Eruption — 127
Inner Healing — 131
Regrets — 134
Roots — 137

Me and My Teddy Bear — 138
Holding Hands With God — 142
A Very Pleasant Interlude — 153
Just Say No — 154

CHAPTER SIX
CONVERGENCE 2008–2012 — 159
J'accuse — 159
For the Plaintiff — 161
The Gorilla In the Room — 177
All I Have to Do Is Dream . . . — 182
Frock You! — 187
Triumph — 190
Now What? — 193
Moment of Silence — 194
Reading the Obituaries — 195
We Interrupt This Program — 197
Here He Lies — 200

AFTERWORD
(To you, if you have been sexually abused)
Victim/Victorious — 203

AUTHOR'S NOTE — 205

ACKNOWLEDGMENTS

Theodore M. Russell, MD, a pediatrician whose personal experience with worried parents and abused children gave him an understanding ear. He spent many hours over several years patiently listening to and corroborating my memories. It is he who convinced me to take action and to write a book for the benefit of others who might be helped to understand their own experience.

Asa Nathanael Russell, MS, LCPC, NCC, my collaborator, who spent many hours reviewing and editing the manuscript; who pressed me to go beyond mere reporting to examining and describing the internal emotional impact of these events.

Terrence Garmey, ESQ, my attorney who also inhabits these pages as a tough but gentle and caring guide who helped me declare my "NO."

Michael Dwinell, MDiv, my therapist about whose wisdom and skill you will read in this book, and who, having helped me uncover my painful memories, died before this manuscript could be finished.

The people of Water of Life Lutheran church in Newcastle, Maine, who lovingly welcomed the teddy bear, which was so important to my recovery.

Nancy Myer Hopkins, MS, and her husband, the Rt. Rev. Harold A. Hopkins, DD, whose extensive experience in this field and sincere interest in the book gave me the courage to suppose it would be of value for the continuing effort to understand, heal, and prevent the scourge of all forms of abuse, particularly in the church.

My children, whose own childhoods were so much affected by these events in unintended ways. Each of them responded to my story with compassion and understanding.

Greta Russell, MDiv, my wife, who lovingly and bravely listened to memories that would be hard for anyone in her position to hear and who consistently encouraged me to include even the hardest parts, in order to tell the whole truth and strive for authenticity.

FOREWORD

This book makes important contributions to the growing field of dealing with sexual exploitation in religious institutions. It takes the reader inside the heart and mind of the narrator and reveals his effort to find understanding and release from a lifelong struggle. It will be helpful not only to individuals, but also to study groups in institutions trying to come to grips with incidents similar to this one. Behind every such event there are many different "stories." This story is particularly well told.

In years of working, sometimes together, on behalf of the Episcopal church and others, we often remarked that clergy abuse is a "contagious ecumenical disease." No religious institution is exempt, and religious institutions are not the only ones vulnerable. A case in point is the current report of the rampant abuse of women in the armed forces. Statistics show that 25% of women—and men also—will be abused during their military careers. There are significant similarities between religious and military institutions in this connection.

It must also be said that sexual abuse by leaders in institutional settings often goes beyond pedophilia, with which the Roman Catholic church has been struggling for years. It can also involve older young people and adults with similar dire impact.

Much is still being learned of this troubling phenomenon from the perspectives of both those who have been abused and those who are recovering abusers. Refusal to maintain the silence is often personally costly, yet many are on the road to recovery and survival. Some are even thriving. What they need is the fundamental understanding and active support of the institutions in which the abuse has taken place. This book is an important part of the examination of that whole process.

It is important to acknowledge that abusive clergy and lay leaders represent only a small percentage of those who work or volunteer in religious settings. We are all grateful for the efforts and success of those who live faithfully and ethically in their various callings. The tasks they face are by no means simple or easy.

Furthermore, contrary to common assumptions, sexual exploitation is not simply about controlling sexual impulses. Rather, sex becomes the instrument of something much more fundamental. Underneath irresponsible and injurious expressions of sexuality lie complex questions of what it means to be a healthy person in wholesome relationships.

Leaders in faith traditions often bear complex symbolism. However, the deepest symbols they must bear are that they become for many, living models both of "holy" humanity and of "The Holy"—two rich but extremely complex, risk-filled roles for anyone to try to uphold. No one completely succeeds at this task, of course. Nevertheless, what we all expect of our church leaders, lay or ordained, is that they not only understand these issues at a deep personal level, but they must also be willing and able to help their people make nourishing connections—not in damaging and narcissistic ways to satisfy *themselves*—but to build healthy relationships to *each other* and ultimately to the One who is truly Holy.

—Nancy Myer Hopkins MS, author, consultant

The Rt. Rev. Harold A. Hopkins, DD, Executive Director of the Office of Pastoral Development of the House of Bishops, Episcopal Church, USA (Ret.)

April 2013 Scarborough, ME

INTRODUCTION

Unfortunately, there are many thousands of others who could write stories like mine. When a child is molested, though it is done in hidden places under the seal of silence, it is not an isolated thing. It cannot be contained but will come out in damaging ways for the rest of at least one life. It is not merely happening to a child; it is happening to the child's family, others whose lives his or her life will touch, and to humanity as a whole.

In this book, I hope to show the broader context that provides cover and opportunity for sexual exploitation to take place. We use this phrase "take place" as a way of saying that something happens. Nothing happens in a vacuum, and my memories are very much connected to the places involved. I have described them in some detail because each led to an unwanted rendezvous.

I am writing about issues of trust, naiveté, denial, deceit, and ignorance—not stupidity, but simply not knowing what needs to be known. What I intend is a glimpse of the many personalities, circumstances, and attitudes that converged to make this abuse possible. Except for the perpetrator, the bishop he attempted to malign, and myself, I have invented names to hide other identities.

Because I have described my experiences in some detail, I strongly advise that young children not have access to this book.

I am a retired Episcopal priest myself, ordained for over fifty years, thirty-five of which I spent in active ministry. This is my frame of reference, and much of what I have written here reflects that. Perhaps it will provide an inside view of the church's life as well as my own, for better and for worse.

—Carl A. Russell, Jr.

Boothbay Harbor, Maine April, 2013

Chapter One

Three Days in May – 1954

Day One

I knew the car well, the big green Chrysler New Yorker careening into sight around the corner, just beyond our house. On a normal day it would not be surprising to see it slowing to turn into our yard, as it did regularly. But today it was reckless as it approached. I was about to reach into our mailbox as I saw the car out of the corner of my eye. It came to a sudden stop beside me. The window slowly lowered. The occupant leaned out and with urgency in his voice said, "If they ask you about *us*, don't tell them anything." The window went up, and the car left me bewildered and frightened. I stood still for several minutes, trying to get my mind around what was happening. A wave of panic was climbing my legs and into my gut. Something solid in me was giving way. I was swallowing air and grasping at some way to get myself under control.

It had been a long time since his last intimate contact with me. I thought it was all behind me. There was a whole lot to "tell," as if I would ever tell. Telling was the last thing I would do. I knew

1

that, above everything, my ability to get on with my life depended on keeping the lid on all of it. My mind darted to a disturbing memory of another occasion when that car and that man had left me standing in this very place in the same state of mind. It was no accident that my mind and my body were responding in this way. I really *had* been here before.

Presently, I realized that the door of the mailbox was still open, the little red metal signal flag still standing in the up position. The bundle of mail remained inside waiting to be retrieved. I had lost track of where I was and what I was there for. Mechanically, I reached in for the mail, closed the door, and returned the flag to its down position.

I scuffed my way up the stained and broken cement walk that led from Route One to my house. In the winter when I had to shovel that walk, it seemed endless. Now I wished it was twice its length. I had to slow things down. I needed to get my thoughts together. How did it get out after such a long time, and how long might it follow me?

How would I explain it? Who are *they?* What are *they* asking? What do *they* know? What kind of trouble am I in? I had just celebrated my seventeenth birthday and was about to go off to college. Now this!

As I approached the house, I decided I would have to pretend that nothing was wrong. I knew how to do that well. I had pretended for ten years that things that had happened over and over again had never happened at all.

My parents were just sitting down for lunch. My father's suit jacket was draped over the back of his chair, as usual. The strong odor of the newly installed linoleum argued with the steaming casserole of my mother's smothered beef. They were exchanging benign details of their morning and making plans for a weekend trip to the neighboring state to visit my great aunt Agnes. Laying the mail on the sideboard with all the calm I could muster, I sat down at the table and passed my plate.

It had been four years since the last episode with him. Yet in an instant, it leaped out from the place where I had successfully hidden it. Here it was with a life revived, demanding silence while it ravaged my inner thoughts. How could I find out more? Could I call him? Would he come back to explain? He never did. That fleeting moment at the mailbox was the last time I ever saw him as my parish priest. The next day, he vanished.

Day Two

I spent my morning rearranging the bedroom I had shared with my two brothers all my life. My oldest brother had married and moved away. My other brother had already left for med school. This was my chance to have the room to myself. I had been low man on the totem pole and, being the youngest by six years, something of a nuisance. Now, I had this space all to myself. It was time to make it my own. I was busy packing boxes to put away under the eaves and rearranging the furniture when my mother called up the stairs to say lunch was ready and that my father was on his way home. I took time to tape another box and grabbed the bottle of cold 7-Up I had been nursing in the eighty-degree heat of this attic room. I went downstairs, helped her carry the meal to the table, and we sat down to wait.

Soon he came through the back door. We could hear him in the kitchen, clearing his throat, then silence. After an anxious interval, he appeared, slowly walking toward the table, his suit coat over his shoulder, his head lowered. My mother watched him expectantly as he drew out his chair and sat down. Something was definitely different today. Did they know what I had known now for twenty-four hours? Were they in on the secret? I knew something was coming and that it would probably involve me.

My father put his head in his hands and began to sob quietly. My mother arose and went to his end of the table. She put her arms around his shoulders.

He seemed inconsolable. We waited quietly. When he recovered, he told the story of his morning.

Having arrived at his office, he was told by his secretary that there was a call for him from the office of the bishop. Being the junior warden of the parish, this was not so unusual. The diocesan office often had business with the senior and junior wardens, who were the lay leaders of the congregation. It is the wardens who are responsible for relations between the people of the congregation and the clergy who serve them. It is they, too, who are expected to deal with any crisis in the rectory—sickness, dereliction, or malfeasance.

He returned the call and was asked by the bishop if he could come, at once, to the diocesan offices. A call had been made to the senior warden, as well, and he was on his way as they spoke. My father returned to his car at the parking garage and drove uptown to the bishop's office. When he was ushered in, he saw his friend the senior warden, the bishop, and the chancellor of the diocese, who was a well-known attorney holding high office in the Eisenhower Administration. My father knew all of *them*, but there was someone else who he had never met.

The bishop spoke first. "We're here because something very serious has happened. I want you to meet John Snelling, the county attorney." They quickly exchanged greetings. This was not a social moment. The bishop continued, "Mr. Snelling, will you please tell the others what you have told me?"

The county attorney nodded his head. "Your rector has been arrested by the city police for providing alcohol to minors. Two young men from the East End were arrested the other night for drunkenness and illegal possession of alcohol. When the detective in charge questioned them, one of the boys blurted out to the other, 'You know where we got it, you fag. I'm not going down with you!' "

The others in the room were standing in stunned silence. "Why don't we sit down," said the bishop. The tension was relieved. The senior warden and the bishop lit cigarettes.

Snelling went on. "The boy was frightened and eager to tell us more. 'Where did you get the alcohol?' 'We got it at the rectory in the next town.' 'How did you know where to get it?' the detective asked. The other boy reluctantly joined in. 'It's not the first time,' he said in a surly tone. 'Anybody can get it if they go along with him.' "

Snelling continued, "We have had suspicions that there is some sort of sex ring centered at your rectory. If it were not for these two boys, we would not have had cause for arrest. As it is, I have enough on him for a grand jury."

The bishop interrupted, "We can't have that! We can't have a scandal like this get into the papers. Is there some way we can avoid that?"

"Not really," said Snelling. "This will be a matter of public record. Reporters read the court docket every day. They'll get it in a day or two. Bishop, what are the church's rules regarding this sort of thing?"

"Well, the Canons *(the guidelines for church order)* say that I can depose *(defrock)* him if the behavior amounts to moral turpitude." The chancellor spoke. "Bishop, I don't think you have any recourse but to depose him."

"But it will have to be published in the national church magazine!" said the bishop.

"Well, there aren't many here who will need to see that," the chancellor replied.

The wardens looked anxiously at the bishop. "What about our parish? This could ruin us," said the senior warden.

"What will the charges be?" asked my father.

"Providing alcohol to minors and lewd conduct with a minor," answered Snelling. There was a long pause while all five men considered the options. The county attorney was arguing with himself silently. He had a duty to perform, but there were powerful men in the room. His was an elected office, and the chancellor was influential in the political arena. A long silence ensued, each man in the room hoping that someone else would come up with a solution.

"What about this?" said Snelling, "If you will depose (defrock) him, I won't bring charges. But here's the deal: he is to leave tonight, and he is not to step foot into this state. If he does, I *will* bring the charges and prosecute him." The five men continued to discuss the pros and cons. There would be many in the diocese who would be very angry at the bishop for deposing him. On the other hand, prosecution and the wide publicity associated with it would be very damaging to everybody involved. It could well be a prolonged case, dragged through the press and compromising the day-to-day life of the parish. It was bad enough to lose their rector, but to be coping with the aftermath day in and day out would be debilitating! Was deposition too harsh a penalty, ruining the life plan of someone who was a major leader in the diocese, who had done good things for the town and for many of its families? There would be hell to pay, no matter what they decided. Silence again.

My father studied the men, wondering what

they might be thinking. By the time the conversation was finished, he knew. The chancellor was focused on the legal standing of the diocese. The bishop was already calculating the what, when, where, and how of his next steps. The wardens were pondering how they would explain this calamity to the parish when Sunday came. There would be speculation and gossip to contend with.

My father interrupted his story to serve more of the haddock my mother had prepared and to pour himself another glass of milk. The table conversation had lulled me into a surprising sense of relief. If my father had known I was involved, he would have told me by now. Listening to his report, my mind pondered the two teenagers whose arrest had begun the unraveling of the story. Curiously, no one mentioned them. They had been bribed with alcohol and then sexually exploited. They were minors; delinquents, yes, but a law had been broken, which was written to protect them, and no one seemed to care about that. The public defender failed to protect these two messed-up members of the public he was charged to defend.

My father went on to tell the rest of the story. The upshot was that the deal was struck and the rector was allowed to walk away from what he had done, untouched by the law, without prosecution. Fifty-four years later he would dismiss it all, writing in his own obituary simply, "God had other plans." He left that day. There would be no final service where he might address the congregation, no explanatory letter, no chance to inform close friends. No one would see him again. It was like a death with no funeral. As for the two boys, they would go to juvenile court. After all, they were nobodies. They had no reputation, except as troublemakers. There was nobody to back them up, nobody to debate the pros and the cons for *them!*

The words "juvenile court" startled me. If these two boys were headed for juvenile court, where was I headed if I was found out? As the story unfolded, it included not only the boys but also sailors picked up by taxi drivers who procured them along the waterfront where the North Atlantic Fleet came and went throughout the Second World War. It was dawning on me that I was part of something terrible. Whatever innocence I might have thought there was in his relationship with me, it had been engulfed in a dark and sordid story. My life of pretending had been part of an elaborate masquerade. I felt dirty and squalid—used, exploited, and betrayed. In my mind I saw a precarious line between getting on with my life and going to jail. These thoughts were weaving a tangled knot in my head, but I was not at liberty to share them with with anyone.

I barely noticed that my father had finished. All was silent except for the sound of muffled sobs. Their beloved rector was gone! They would never see him again. He would never sit at this very table where they had laughed and shared and learned so much, where their mutual admiration had flourished. There we were, seated around the table, their sobs breaking the silence. If they knew what *I* was hiding, what would be happening just now? Would their grief turn to anger? And who would they be angry at? Would it be him or me? I could not chance that. So a chasm divided us that would never be bridged for as long as they lived.

Day Three

On the same day the rector was spirited away, I received a personal call from the bishop. He asked me to meet with him in his office the next morning, day three. I was an Aspirant for Holy Orders, which brought me under the bishop's jurisdiction. This came about because by age twelve, I had concluded that I wanted to be ordained myself. The complex reasons that led to this early aspiration become clearer as my story unfolds, but I was encouraged by a lot of positive reinforcement. As soon as I had whispered the idea of being ordained, I was showered with attention. People registered delight. I was told that I had a *calling*, what a wonderful priest I would be, why, perhaps I could even be a bishop one day! Furthermore it was a feather in the cap of any congregation to be "sending a son into the ministry." So by now, at seventeen, I was on track to enter college in the fall as a pre-theological student. To reach my goal of ordination, I would be required to satisfy the expectations of many people—the bishop, the standing committee, my seminary dean, the faculty, the examining chaplains, and others that I hadn't even heard of yet. It would take seven years. But at this early stage, the bishop could put an end to it all, here and now!

The silence of the night unleashed a storm of worry. I lay in the dark imagining what this meeting would be like. It would most certainly involve some sort of interrogation. How would I keep the secret safe? I was also beginning to feel some of the grief I had seen in my parents the day before. Such an abrupt ending to it all, the good and the bad! Sadness, relief, anger, fear—all of them were racing through my mind.

In the morning, I reluctantly drove the six miles from home to the diocesan office in the family car. I had no idea what the bishop had in mind. I just wanted it all to go away, to get it over with, one way or the other. I sat nervously outside his office. The sound of the secretary's manual typewriter seemed to be tapping out my own staccato thoughts. What if ... If only ... What now ...? I heard voices from the other side of his door. They must be talking about me. Was the county attorney in there?

The door opened, and there stood the bishop. He ushered me into his office, where my father had met with him the day before. The phantom voice had disappeared. I sat across the desk and felt as if the bishop's eyes were scanning my own secret files. "Thank you for coming in, Carl. I have a few questions I would like to ask you." I nodded my head but said nothing. I was feeling queasy and a little light-headed. "What did you know about the things that have happened with your rector?" He stopped and left me in silence.

In that moment I had a choice—a choice I would encounter many times in my future. This was an interrogation to implicate me in the crime that had led to the defrocking of the rector and sent the other boys involved to court. Clearly, from what I could see, the message was that anyone who had been involved in such a scandal was more likely to be jailed than ordained. If I told him the truth, I would be part of the "moral turpitude," and I was sure that I would be declared unfit for ordination. It never occurred to me that he might be asking because of a concern for my own welfare. It is likely that he was inquiring to discover the effect of this crisis on my own sense of vocation. If I *had* been involved, would it not be important to give me the benefit of counseling to make sense of it all before it contaminated the rest of my life? As I look back, I think of how different things might have been if my own mind were not locked in flight mode. How different it would have been if I had told the bishop the truth and received the help I needed then. But I truly believed that, for my own safety, I could not tell anyone anything. So, I lied. I said, "Well, I know from what my father has told me, but that is all."

"Did he ever involve you in any of this?" he continued.

"No," I lied again.

"Are you sure?" he asked.

"I am very sure," I said. Three times a liar!

The bishop sat back in his chair, his hands laid palm down on his desk. He looked me in the eye. I diverted my eyes to look past his shoulder at the traffic passing by on the busy street. Even when things are hanging in the balance, life keeps moving on. The syncopated tapping of the typewriter was audible in the silence. What was he pondering? Had I been convincing in my deceit? Had he been told something more that he was holding back to see if I would come clean with him? What about the rector? Had *he* told what he had ordered me *never* to tell? I had no way of knowing what had transpired between him and the bishop when the sentence of deposition had been delivered. Perhaps he had been coerced into divulging all the hapless players in his covert world. I had no way of knowing.

A voice whispered insistently just then in my imagination. The *other* one who knew about us; had *she* told? Had she been so frightened for herself, so burdened by what she knew of the inner life of the rectory, that she had purged her troubled soul to the investigators questioning her? There was a lot at stake for her. She was about to lose her home, her livelihood, the future she supposed she would have in the rector's household. Why *wouldn't* she cooperate freely if pressed for answers? This inner conversation taunted me as I determined to keep the silence the bishop had begun. Finally he spoke. "Well, I am happy to hear that. I was hoping he had not involved you." What a relief! I smiled reassuringly, as if there were not squirrels doing somersaults in my chest. I could tell he was relieved, too. This was not something he would have to deal with any further in my case. He brought the interview to an end, shook my hand, and wished me well in my first year of college.

I closed the door of the diocesan house and stood at the top of the steps, listening to the rush of traffic as it moved toward the intersection of Main and Congress. Things were converging. My abuser had been dispatched in twenty-four hours. No one had said a word about *us*. The secret was safe for now, but I was left alone with the truth. I had a future to protect from the past with which my abuser had marked me, all of it intersecting across the bishop's desk like the traffic merging at the corner. Already my feelings were being driven inward, bottled up, and I was screwing the lid on tight. It had been only three days, but the story behind the story, the truth with which I was left to contend, had begun ten years before.

Chapter Two

Backstory 1944–1954

'Tis the Gift to Be Simple
In 1943, when I was seven, our family attended the Second Congregational Church on the backside of town. My mother's father had been a founding deacon, and she had grown up there. When she and my father married, he joined her. From 1923 to 1944, while my parents' lives were being woven into a family, the life of that Congregational Church was a major thread. It is where nearly all of their friendships were formed and where my brothers and I were baptized. Many of my happy memories are the fruit of our years there, where membership and friendship mingled.

Both my parents were musicians. My father had trained in Boston and New York to sing opera. At some point in the process, his voice teacher took him aside and kindly advised him that it was unlikely he would ever succeed professionally but that, with his fine voice, he should make his impact by returning to his hometown to encourage music locally. As a young man, with my mother as his accompanist, he entertained audiences singing sacred concerts. He became the director of the church choir. Rehearsals were informal and often planned around potluck suppers at our home. On those occasions, I went to bed and heard them laughing and singing downstairs. My mother's sewing circle also met at our home. During those afternoons I would play behind the living room sofa and listen to these friends chatter as they made bandages for soldiers wounded at the front line in Europe during WWII.

On Sundays, my parents were seated with the choir during worship. My brothers and I sat with our nana, who always carried a satchel full of coloring papers, pencils, and crayons for me to use during the service. I felt safe there, always safe. The church building was sparse, methodically designed to be as plain as possible so as to avoid all "distractions" from the pulpit, which stood squarely at the center of the platform. Clear glass windows provided an open view to the trees and lawns outside. There was no stained glass. Music was accompanied by a standard Hammond organ like the ones I heard on the soap operas my grandmother listened to, sitting by her Philco console radio. In short, my parents were plain people whose history and culture placed them in a simple setting where they were admired and respected.

But seeds of change were being planted by my oldest brother. He was part of a Boy Scout troop that met at the Episcopal Church only ten minutes walk from our house. He and another scout were befriended by the rector, who frequently dropped in on the weekly meetings. They began to spend a good deal of time at the rectory, so much time, in fact, that my father became concerned about the inordinate amount of attention given to them by the bachelor minister. There were those who whispered that the rectory was not a safe place for children. Being acquainted with the other scout's father, a prominent surgeon, my father called to ask if there might be some reason to be concerned about this involvement. The doctor replied, "They're big boys, Carl. They can take care of themselves." That was not an answer, but since my father stood in awe of the medical community, around the edges of which he worked professionally, the response settled his mild suspicions and lulled him into a relieved disinterest.

It was customary for the troop to attend the church in uniform on Boy Scout Sunday. The parents of nonmembers were invited to accompany their sons. Since the family still attended the Congregational Church, my parents attended as guests. Soon my brother announced that he would no longer be attending the Congregational Church with the family. He had taken an interest in this more formal church and began attending it by himself. However, it became apparent that it was not the church alone that attracted him. A girl had caught his eye. She would later become his wife.

During this time, my mother was caring for her own mother, who was no longer strong enough to live alone in the old homestead. As Nana was approaching the time of her death, my brother asked the rector to visit and say prayers with her. Though he was not our pastor, he agreed to make the visit. He was particularly gifted at this sort of pastoral care, and my mother found great comfort in his manner and the things he said and did. He brought with him a small vial of oil and, putting on a special purple stole, he conferred the Sacrament of Holy Unction for the sick and dying. He spoke in quiet and assuring tones. Slowly and deliberately he dipped his thumb in the oil. Then he gently traced a cross on her forehead, saying;

> *"Nellie, I anoint you in the Name*
> *of the Father and of the Son and*
> *of the Holy Ghost. Amen."*

This was something my family had never witnessed.

There was no such ritual in their Congregational Church. No color, no stoles, no prayers from a book; *simple* was the adjective in their church life. By contrast, that quiet moment of anointing with oil carried with it a mystique, something out of the ordinary to which they were so accustomed. It carried them beyond the moment at hand toward something greater, something beyond them, a promise for her that gave them hope. In a few days Nana lay dying. This time it was my father who called for him to come. He came promptly and, as before, he took her hand in his and spoke to her quietly but firmly, more a declaration than a prayer:

> *Depart, O Christian soul, out of this world, in the Name of God, the Father Almighty who created thee. In the Name of Jesus Christ, who redeemed thee. In the Name of the Holy Ghost who sanctifieth thee. May thy rest be this night in peace, and thy dwelling place in the Paradise of God. Amen.*

"Dwelling place." "Paradise of God." The words echoed in the silence, repeating themselves in our thoughts—soothing, comforting, encouraging, painting a mural in our minds that gave hope and settled our very troubled hearts.

After that interval of quiet, he invited us to gather around her bed. Placing his hand on her forehead, he prayed;

> *Into thy hands, O merciful Savior, we commend the soul of thy servant, Nellie, now departed from the body. Acknowledge, we humbly beseech thee, a sheep of thine own fold, a lamb of thine own flock, a sinner of thine own redeeming. Receive her into the arms of thy mercy, into the blessed rest of everlasting peace, and into the glorious company of the saints in light. Amen. (Book of Common Prayer 1928)*

I was part of this moment. I stood there next to my Nana's bed watching, listening. My precious Nana, who had tended me so many times at the Congregational Church; we were losing her. This was the first time I had ever witnessed a death. I was sad and worried as I saw my parents crying. I felt like somebody needed to do something, yet there was nothing *I* could do; but the rector *did* have something to do, something to say, touching their shoulders, taking their hands, speaking softly but confidently. It was a deeply significant moment, and I watched as this man brought comfort and peace to my parents and me. There was strength and a mystical sense of presence in what he did. This was something I wanted to do someday. I wanted to be like him.

He prayed with us, as well, laying his hand on our foreheads, the first time a minister had ever touched me. Then he quietly left. The impact of those moments never left any of us. My parents recounted them for years to come. God had touched our hearts, and the rector had been the instrument. His visits became more and more frequent. He would arrive with his briefcase and, when supper was over, join the family in the living room, conversing while he red-penciled articles submitted for the Northeast, the diocesan magazine, of which he was the editor. He was a powerful and charismatic presence, held in high esteem. I could see that he was becoming special to us. My mother and father deferred to him, asked him questions, and sought his counsel. But although we were befriending him, I knew he had not yet become our pastor. We were still attending the Congregational Church.

Migration

Soon after my Nana died, my mother fell into a deep depression. Fatigue took a heavy toll. Her grief was intensified by the loss of the home in which she had been born, now inherited by her brother. That house held the memories of her childhood—the hours she spent in the barn with her pet donkey, the horse she had loved so much, which had carried her to church and stores and family outings, her childhood dream of farming the land. She often spoke of these things, sharing the stories of her childhood, even a poem she had written as a young girl about how she *would* farm the land one day. All the hope of that expired with her mother's final breath. Sadness, disappointment, and fatigue mingled to rob us of the architect of our home life. For several weeks she was not herself, and it felt to me as if a big part of her had left us. I missed her very much, thinking this was how it might always be.

The rector came by from time to time, and his care and concern seemed to lift my mother's burden. He brought wise counsel and patient understanding, and these ushered her to a brighter outlook. She slowly regained her usual serene and loving self, as if she were returning from a faraway journey and joining us once more. It was a gift for us, and we all knew that it was the rector who had figuratively taken her hand and led her home to us. My father and mother decided that it was time to try the Episcopal Church just down the road.

I was glad. As I look back, I wonder at this decision. They left that familiar society, of which they had been a part for so many years and migrated to something radically different. In many ways it was a jarring culture shock. There was no falling out, as is so often the case. They did not take offense at the minister or his message. There was no church fight in which they had become embroiled on the losing side. That had happened when "Second Parish" had left "First Parish" and built its own church across town. No, it was something else—not something that drove them *away* from the one, but something that attracted them *to* the other.

There had been generations of Congregationalists on my mother's side and Methodists on my father's side. Each of these denominations had contested the traditions and authority of the Church of England in the seventeenth century. For reasons that made sense at the time, these societies eliminated most of the Catholic influence that had been retained in the Church of England. Ironically, things were coming full circle. What my parents were experiencing now in the Episcopal Church were the form and structure of which they had been deprived by their own histories. When they happened upon it, they were captivated. In the rector, they found it embodied in a form they had never known, and it opened to them a whole new world—an opportunity for a whole new identity. It was a conversion experience in which they left behind everything familiar—their friends, their positions, their influence—and made a new beginning.

In the Beauty of Holiness

The first Sunday we attended the new church made a significant impression on me, one that affected the rest of my life. I had seen the impressive building from a distance before we left the Congregational Church because nearby was a little "Mom and Pop" store where my father filled the tank of his company car. This store was a focal point of much joy in my school days. It was one of the bookends that stood at the edges of a beautiful grove of Norway pines, the other being the elementary school that I attended from grade 1 to grade 5. Both of them were near enough to my home that I was able to walk to them.

On fine days at lunchtime, we were allowed to walk from the school, through the sunlit grove, to the store where we would buy penny candy, half pints of strawberry milk, or my favorite, Dixie Cups in vanilla, chocolate, or strawberry. First, I would find the little wooden spoon on the bottom. Then

I would lick the back of the cover, revealing the picture on the inside, usually a popular movie star. Comparing my picture with those of my friends, I would delight in eating my way back through the pines to our afternoon of classes. The majesty of the trees, the aroma of the soft-fallen needles, and the fresh salt air from the bay filled me with light-hearted joy. I had hardly noticed the towering stone building across the busy highway. Now, it was my church.

Built of shimmering red-stone granite, it soared above the surrounding landscape. My father, who had served in the navy in WWI, laid out a nautical chart to show me the little round circle with a dot in the middle indicating our new church as a landmark that guided the North Atlantic Fleet entering the harbor during the Second World War. No other building in our town was high enough to have that distinction.

As a little boy, walking toward it on the flagstone path from the highway that first morning, it loomed high and majestic. Its solid granite walls, with notches cut intermittently into the top, looked like a huge castle rising out of the earth. My eyes followed the tower upward to the very top, where I spied a huge, bronze weather vane, a rooster perched on the cross trees pointing north, south, east, and west. The billowing clouds moving across the blue sky made me dizzy. The great tower appeared to be toppling. It was truly awesome!

Inside, the church was dark and cool. In exchange for transparency, the beautiful stained-glass windows transformed the common light of day into splendid shafts of deep blue and crimson, yellows and greens, depicting images of the Virgin Mary, Prophets, Apostles, and Martyrs. I had never seen anything like this! It was a revelation of beauty. This was something so set apart from the familiar in my life that it was like walking into another world. I was entering holy space. As my eyes adjusted to the interior, I saw beautiful oak prayer desks and choir stalls, hand carved in delicate trefoils. Light reflected off the polished rose marble of the altar in a soft glow, accented by the simple lines of the carved oak paneling behind it. Tall candles flickered across the paneling, making tiny mesmerizing points of light that skittered across the static wall.

I sat in the chapel chair next to my father. I'm sure there must have been shuffling of chairs, kneelers being scuffed into place, people clearing their throats—all the sounds of a church in expectation of the beginning of worship. But I don't remember hearing any of that. I was *feeling* the silence deep within me. Then I heard the quiet, breathy tones of woodwinds, and my whole body resonated with the deep, powerful, undergirding bass of the pipe organ filling the expansive space. As I listened, I realized it came from *above* us. To my young mind it seemed like heaven had opened. It was as if fragile strings, which had been waiting in my inner self, were humming with life as these outer strings of beauty and color and sound were plucked around me. At age seven! There were no words to describe it.

Soon the worship began. Everyone stood up. As they joined in singing, I became aware of movement down the aisle from behind us. I looked back and saw a cross, carried by an older boy in gloved hands. Two young boys carried candles. They were all wearing long red robes with shorter white coverings. The choir walked behind them. *They* were wearing long *black* robes with white coverings, a startling contrast with the choir my father had led at the Congregational Church. The Congregational choir dressed in street clothes like everybody else.

After the choir came the rector. I had never seen him like this. When he came to our house, he was dressed in black with a high clerical collar around his neck. Now he was dressed in a long white robe with a beautiful, colorful poncho hanging front and back from his shoulders to his knees.

The pageantry gave a sense of dramatic movement within the singularly significant space around us. The procession sang its way to the front, and the participants took their places on each side, facing each other. They were singing across the space that had made such a great impact on me. This was my first experience of the Sublime.

The Opera He Never Sang

My father was infatuated by it all. Like many converts, he was determined to practice this religion to a fault. Driving me to school, as we passed the church, he would raise his hat to acknowledge and honor the Reserved Sacrament, communion bread reverently placed in a little safe in the wall beside the altar, to be brought to the sick, the shut-in, and the dying. There, a candle burned night and day to note the Presence of Christ. At the time I didn't know this. Sitting in the car beside him, I saw my father tip his hat to the church and everything that happened there.

The nomenclature, too, had captured his attention. He set about learning this new culture, the building in which every part had a name, and even the special clothing the rector wore. He was particularly taken by the black cassock with purple piping and buttons, over which he wore a shoulder cape lined with crimson taffeta, the bishop's color, signifying that he was a Canon of the Cathedral. On his head he wore a square hat with three ridges, each with crimson piping and sporting a crimson pom-pom on top, a biretta. We had never seen anything like it.

In 1944 the whole family was confirmed on the same Sunday, except for me. I was considered too young to understand, though I had been deeply moved by my experience, perhaps more so than any of the others. I had been urgent in my plea to be included with everyone else, but the rule was that no one could take the confirmation vows until at least twelve years old. I would have to wait five more years for my turn. They all got up, left the row, and stood in the aisle. I sat in the empty row, feeling very much left out, and watched them go forward, one by one, to kneel at the feet of the bishop. He was seated in a special chair placed at the steps that led to the altar. He was wearing a crimson robe with a heavy gold cross around his neck and a pointed hat in the shape of flame, symbolizing his connection with the first apostles upon whom the Holy Spirit came in tongues of fire. He carried an ornate staff, shaped like a shepherd's crook, to reflect his position as shepherd of the flock. Over his shoulders was draped a colorful tapestry cape embroidered with cloth of gold. As they knelt there, the bishop laid his hands firmly on each head, looked them in the eye, and spoke these impressive words. As he said them over my father, I claimed them for my own:

Defend, O Lord, this Thy child, Carl, with Thy Heavenly Grace, that he may continue Thine forever; and daily increase in Thy Holy Spirit more and more, until he come unto Thine Everlasting Kingdom. Amen.

I sat there wanting so much for those words to be said for me! From that moment I knew them by heart. I said them for myself many times, even as a little boy. I repeated them aloud when I was raking or mowing lawns. They were engraved on my mind. I have carried them all through my life. I often say them when I am frightened or before I go to sleep. As I tended the dying in my own congregations, I would bend close to speak them softly in their ear, and both they and I were comforted by them. Ritual words like these are full of power. Our new church gave us many such tools of faith to cherish.

Mirror, Mirror

Why was my father so enchanted by this man? Surely no one can be what my father reckoned the rector to be. There was something buried in my father that this man was able to reflect. There were many reasons for my father to feel inadequate. Unlike both of his brothers, he had dropped out of college. For years, until I was a grown man, I was under the impression that he had left college to return home to care for his ailing father. In fact, he had left for a less admirable reason—he was lovesick for his girlfriend back home.

He often compared himself unfavorably to very close friends—his childhood pal who had become a physician, college-educated business associates, people who I knew lacked anything like his own integrity, wisdom, and strength of character. Yet, in spite of his low self-esteem, the community looked up to him. He was sought out for advice and leadership in the organizations of which he was a part. He was in charge of civilian defense in our town during the war. He tried his own cases before the state insurance commission before lawyers got a law passed to make that illegal. My cousins called him for counsel when things like divorce or infidelity invaded their lives. When his boss suffered a total paranoid breakdown in the office, it was my father who managed the situation. I knew all these things. There was much to be admired about him. Yet he was convinced, as I heard him repeat so many times, he would "never amount to anything."

Dr. Carl Jung argues that as we form a sense of self in a highly structured culture, we are forced to deny aspects of ourselves. There are dark things that culture requires us to abandon, such as aggression and moral taboos. But there are also highly significant and good things that are also discouraged, which may be thought of as our "gold." As we make overt choices about our lives and how we will live them and who we will be, we are also choosing *not* to be something else. The collection of these other possibilities becomes hidden from our awareness. Our gold is made up of the unrealized potential we possess but cannot or will not access.

In his book, *Owning Your Own Shadow*, Robert Johnson writes,

> I have written of the shadow as the dark, unacceptable part of oneself. But I also have noted that it is possible to project from the shadow the very best of oneself onto another person or situ-

ation. Our hero-worshipping capacity is pure shadow; in this case our finest qualities are refused and laid on another. It is hard to understand, but we often refuse to bear our own noble traits and instead find a shadow substitute for them.*

It *is* hard for us to accept and affirm the good things about us. By the time we have heard our parents scolding us when we are naughty, the church telling us we are all miserable sinners, and children inhabiting the playground at recess mocking and teasing us, this information gets pretty deeply written into our brains. We become suspicious of the "gold" residing in our inner selves. Then someone comes along who is just the person we would like to be. In situations such as the one that evolved with the rector and my father, there is a harmonic resonance in which the need for adulation in the one provides the screen from which the repressed attributes of the other will be brightly reflected. When this happens and when it is encouraged by the inner need of the other to be adored, it becomes pathological. This projection, which is larger than life,

*Robert S. Johnson, *Owning Your Own Shadow*, (San Francisco: Harper, 1991), 42, ISBN number 0-06-250422-3. Available at Amazon.com.

comes to govern and determine the behavior of the person in my father's role.

I believe that my father had a deep longing to be somebody more than he was. He had attempted to realize it through a professional life in opera and had failed. Now he had found the perfect mirror in the rector. It resulted in an unquestioning trust and a willingness to defer to and overestimate the man who "could do no wrong." These are the ingredients that often result in cults. They clearly resulted in a dangerous circumstance for me.

Accordingly, my father wanted to highlight the rector in every way. After becoming the junior warden of the parish, a position that placed him in charge of the property, he installed a powerful spotlight to highlight the rector in the pulpit. A new ritual was inaugurated with the rector's hearty approval. During the sermon hymn, the lights in the nave and all the altar and chancel lights were dimmed. As the rector mounted the pulpit steps, the brightness of the spotlight was raised to feature him while he preached. Furthermore, as a child sitting in our usual place in the congregation, the light against the stucco background of the chancel wall gave the impression that he actually had a halo around his head like the saints in a Raphael painting. It worked for me. I really thought this man must *be* a saint. What my father saw before him were the repressed and hidden virtues he could not realize in himself. It never occurred to the rector to help my father *recover* his gold and own the best parts of himself.

The Newly Minted Key

One Saturday morning, my father recruited me to help him in one of his many church projects. We drove into the churchyard and stopped by the tower entrance. Access to the tower was through a diminutive oak door, which was kept locked to most, except the rector, the sexton, the organist, and my father. We unloaded wires, electrical boxes, sockets, tubing, and tools, along with a high-capacity dehumidifier, and headed across the lawn to the little door. My father handed me a newly minted key on a labeled key chain. He said, "You will be needing this now. Go ahead. Try it. *You* open the door." This was something special. There were only four people who had a key to that door. Now there were five! The key worked. I opened the door, and in we went. We were headed for the rooms high above the worship space. This meant climbing the ninety steps of the Great Tower, which ascended inside an octagonal stone tube married to one corner of the main building.

Inside, it was dark and musty. Light clawed its way through narrow slits in the one-foot thick stone wall. Grated iron steps were stacked like Lego® blocks, creating a spiral stairway that led to two interior levels. Our shoes, scuffing up the iron steps, stirred up a ringing that could be heard from top to bottom. Our destination was the organ chamber on the first level. Here was the practical machinery of the instrument that had filled the worship space with the sublime music that had so affected me on that first Sunday. The first thing I came to was the biggest electric motor I had ever seen. It drove a blower attached to the organ by a large, flexible hose. There were wind chests, cables, and large, wooden bass pipes laid on their sides, like stacked cordwood. Myriad metal pipes stood in formation like fusiliers, dropped into their designated sockets in the wind chests. On the floor were cast-off pipes, short lengths of wire, and dried-out leathers—detritus left from repairs of the past. From one end of the room to the other, a wooden walkway traversed a very large grated hole cut in the floor to let the sound of the organ pass through and float down to the congregation below.

When I walked across that bridge and looked down through the grate, I felt the impressive height of the chamber in the pit of my stomach. I leaned over the rail and stared at the chapel chairs arranged in perfect rows sixty feet below. I had never been at such a height in my life. At one corner of the chamber, a bundled coaxial cable threaded its way across the floor, disgorging hundreds of lesser wires, each finding its way to a single electrical valve that admitted wind from the chest. This would waken a slumbering pipe to sound its note on demand from the organ console below. I realized I was actually *inside* an instrument.

The cable passed through the tower to tumble along the outside wall of stone until it reached the foundation of the building. From there it made its way through the damp basement to emerge by the organ console at the front of the church. Exposure to the elements in the heat and humidity of summer and the icy cold of winter resulted in moisture, causing unwanted short circuits that sounded pipes out of order and at embarrassing moments during worship. My father called these moments ciphers. This was the reason for the dehumidifier. We spent the day installing it at the place where the cable departed the organ chamber as a way of preventing the ciphers. When we were finished, it hummed away in its place, sponging the unwanted moisture from the air.

Then my father said, "I have a surprise for

you." He sent me alone back to the tower steps. Climbing twenty more steps, I found myself in the belfry. Dozens of pigeons flushed into the air, their wings stirring up dust and molted feathers everywhere. When the flurry settled, I stepped into the cold, drafty room. Wind swept around me from tall, louvered Norman arches. In the middle of the cavernous room a huge bell hung, with a giant wheel attached. On its mounting frame, it stood twice as tall as I was. The only fixture in the room, it was awesome.

I gingerly made my way to peer out through the louvered arches of stone. From there I could see the bay and the islands beyond. Dozens of naval vessels were scattered about the harbor. The North Atlantic Fleet was in. As I stood looking, I heard behind me a rhythmic rattling. My father was pulling the rope, which was threaded from the giant wheel down to the organ chamber. The three-thousand pound mass of cast bronze began to swing. Slowly, back and forth, it gained its momentum, and the arc of its swing increased. I put my fingers in my ears. With creaking and whooshing, the lip struck the clapper and the whole room shook! Now I knew why I had heard the bell so many years before I ever saw it. I could hear it from our house as it peeled its calls to worship long before this was our church. I heard it on days of national celebration like the Fourth of July. I heard it on the morning of May 8, 1945, the day that victory in Europe was announced to the world, VE Day. It was the only bell in our town.

The House with the Funny Name

As my grammar school classmates and I walked the pine grove at lunchtime, we could spy a brown house camouflaged behind the trees near the church across the road. As we wondered about it, one said, "O yeah, that's the house with the funny name. I think it's a rookery or something like that." Eventually, when it was *our* church, I got to see the house with the funny name up close. It was set apart from the church by spacious lawns and gardens, surrounded by groves of pine and spruce trees. Faux beams and multipaned windows punctuated its stuccoed and shingled outside walls. Situated at the end of a long, curving fieldstone walk and bordered by mature hedges, it was barely noticeable from the road.

The big summer event of the parish was an annual parish fair held on the church grounds. It was popular in town and always well attended. As part of the festivities, the rector hosted an open house in his home, which was called the rectory. We all got to do a walk around and take in the style and décor, like attending the Queen's Garden party but on a small scale. Each year the rector surprised his visitors with elaborate floral arrangements displayed in the toilet bowls of his house, with the secondary result that, of course, no one could actually use them. This was the talk of the town.

When my mother had finished her turn at the white elephant table, we made the tour ourselves. We walked the gravel driveway leading from the church to the house and up the fieldstone walk to the ample entry porch and on through a pair of oak doors opening into a beautiful foyer. The sun from the windows at the landing of a grand staircase blinded my eyes as we entered to find others making their way through the house. To the right was the dining room with its heavy velour, pale green drapes, matched by upholstered chairs that nested under a large cherry table. It was furnished for entertaining guests in a formal way, which accounted for the butler's pantry connecting it to the kitchen. Opposite the dining room, across the foyer, was a window-wrapped study looking out over the front gardens. At the foot of the stairs, we turned into the living room. Its damask drapes framed multiple windows at the far end, opening onto the grounds, admitting abundant light. In the center of the room, facing the fireplace was a large sofa accompanied by two wing-backed chairs, facing one another across the coffee table. Next to the windows was a sideboard with fine silver candlesticks, a delicate porcelain bowl, and two decanters of sherry, dark and light. On the mantle were a triptych of the Holy Family and a Greek icon of the trinity. A copy of the thirteenth-century Duccio "Madonna and Child" hung over the fireplace. The tender sadness of the Madonna's eyes, looking at the upheld arm of her child, spilled over the frame, falling on the sofa. Her gaze filled the room. A Mashhad Persian carpet with its deep shades of red and blue lay on the polished oak floors.

As we moved on, we came to the broad carpeted stairs with beautiful varnished railings, leading to a wide landing and on to the upstairs rooms. The door was open to the rector's own bedroom. As the group peered in, they seemed fascinated by this opportunity to invade his privacy. They behaved as if it were a little bit naughty. Then on to the guest room and the bathroom, where the toilet bowl blossomed in a blaze of glory! The housekeeper's quarters in the back rooms were closed to the public. Taken as a whole, the house expressed the refined and tasteful imprint of its chief occupant, the thirty-year-old bachelor Anglican rector who presided over the life of this congregation of affluent residents from the Foreside. I walked the pathway that led back to the church, pondering the beauty of the rectory where *he* lived and the plainness of our own house, which had no name at all.

Shrine

We had very few valuable possessions. One was particularly precious to my mother. It was a finely made, beautifully carved gate leg table that she had inherited when her mother died. Fashioned from American black walnut, it had occupied the formal parlor of her own place of birth. Now, standing at one end of *our* living room, it was a place set apart. There, my mother arranged the few precious artifacts she had brought with her from her own home when she had married my father. The featured one was a black leather portfolio with inlays of mother-of-pearl placed so that it stood against the raised drop leaf of the table propped against the wall by the stairs. In the portfolio were some worn pages of a letter written by her mother and several locks of golden hair, cropped from my mother when she was a little girl. This was not a place where you would place your phone or radio. Those occupied more mundane spaces—the phone on the Singer sewing machine cabinet, and the radio in the old Victrola console. No, the gate leg table was treated with reverent care.

One Christmas, the rector presented my parents with a framed portrait of himself, taken by Bachrach of Boston. Much was made of the Bachrach name signed in gold in the lower right hand corner of the print. My father told how people of great importance were photographed in the Bachrach studio in Boston—presidents, statesmen, physicians of renown, Wall Street barons. People like my parents had daguerreotypes of their parents on the walls or Brownie Camera prints in carefully bound photo albums. But this was a Bachrach! Of course, it belonged on the gate leg table—holy space that displayed only the things that were treasured by my family. The language was unmistakable; he had become an icon, an irrefutable oracle.

As if to punctuate this, on one occasion, having been taught in Confirmation Class about the importance of keeping meatless Fridays, my father came home to find my mother preparing hamburger for our supper. There was a stirring in the kitchen. My father went to the phone to call the rector. I listened to him explain my mother's mistake. Then, *my father* asked *this man* if it would be all right to serve this food at *our table*! Nobody else had ever been consulted about the things we ate. What was a child to *make* of the man who had the power to permit or forbid my father feeding his family the ordinary food my mother had prepared? My own father was positioned in the hierarchy of things below and in submission to the one who bore the *title* "Father."

What Are We Doing Here?

It all began with a kiss. I was sick in bed. The light on the ceiling raced away from me, becoming like a speck in the sky. Then suddenly, the whole ceiling collapsed, as if the sky were falling in. The fixture grew huge, like a meteor coming to crush me. Over and over this happened. For a day and a night I was delirious. Lying in that bed, it was real and terrifying. I was in the clutches of scarlet fever. My mother wrapped me in cool, moistened towels and I was made to swallow glasses of water mixed with something called hydriotic acid. I was weak, and terrified that the delirium would happen to me again.

The loving parish priest, who had been such a comfort to my mother when her mother was near death, came to visit and to pray with *me*. I was upstairs in the bedroom I shared with my brothers. No one else was there at the time. He came and held my hand as he prayed comforting words to allay my fear and to ask God's healing for my sickness. Then he did something he had not done with my nana. He bent over and tenderly kissed me—on my lips. It seemed to be a kindness at the time, a gesture of affection and consolation, much as my mother had done every night of my life. After all, what else does a kiss mean to a young child? But I would learn that there are kisses and then there are *kisses*.

Not long after I recovered, I was selected for acolyte training. At age nine, I would be the youngest acolyte in the parish, a special exception. My older brothers were also acolytes. We were part of a very elite and small number of boys, handpicked by the rector. I was about to be ushered into the inner sanctum, the sacristy. Even the *word* portended something mystical, hidden, and holy. It was all of that.

When I entered, it was like stepping into a completely other world. The light of day was foreign in this shadow of a room. In anticipation of the stained-glass window that would one day be installed, small opaque tiles of colored glass filled the leaded arched spaces. As I stepped through the heavy oak door, I could smell something strange, not quite the same as what I smelled in the big public library. Not like the study in the home of Mr. Pinkham, the old Town Clerk, who sat behind his antique rolltop desk smoking his Sherlock Holmes pipe when I went with my father to pay the excise tax on his car. Venturing further into this unfamiliar place, I discovered that the peculiar smell was the aroma of unburned incense, beeswax candles, oiled oak, old books, the oriental carpet, brass polish, and aging vestments, all blended with the musty air from the dirt cellar beneath.

A broad set of shallow drawers was marked with different colored swatches of cloth to indicate the color of the Eucharistic vestments, carefully laid out between muslin protective coverings. Above these drawers was a beautifully carved locked door. Here, the precious vessels were kept—the ornate gold-lined silver chalice, made from jewelry donated by the Foreside parishioners, silver cruets, and a small silver plate used to distribute communion at the altar rail. On either side of the drawers were two large cabinets. In one were the acolyte vestments. In the other were all the rest of the paraphernalia required to keep the holy house in order—boxes of beeswax candles, the long-handled taperers used to light them at the altar, waxes, polishing cloths, basins, soaps, and sponges. Here was a peculiar mixture of items, to some of which were attached highly religious significance, along with the mundane, to which no significance was attached whatsoever. It was a startling distinction, marked only by the spaces to which they were assigned and the manner in which they were handled.

Training to be an acolyte required learning the names and purposes for all of these. It also involved a particular choreography. For services to move smoothly, certain things had to be done gracefully and with finesse. The wax taperer was carried ever so carefully, a hand cupped to shield the fragile flame as we moved to the altar. There, it was slowly raised to kiss the altar candles, passing its flame along to them. The charred dead wicks came to life standing as the Light of Christ. These were the lights that had danced across the carved paneling on my very first Sunday. The Altar Book, from which the priest read the Holy Writings and the Liturgy itself, was to be lifted high as it was moved from one side of the altar to the other, depending on what was being read. Bread was carried from the Credence Table to the altar. Silver cruets, filled with wine and water, were brought to the priest to be poured into the chalice. Without these elements there would be no communion. Their importance could not be overestimated. Therefore, we were to carry out these otherwise mundane actions so as to embody their dignity and convey their holy significance.

When these had been completed, we carried a large offering plate, holding it against our chest, its glistening interior facing outward, and stood at the foot of the altar steps, waiting to receive the offerings of the people brought to us by the ushers. We were the footmen at a very important feast at which the rector was the majordomo. For every move he made, there was a corresponding move for the acolyte, sort of like a dance. No other unordained person was permitted behind the altar rail. We were regularly reminded that acolytes were special, an order of the church dating back to the third century. It would be many years before "lay people" were included in the ritual.

As part of my training, I was assigned to the late service in tandem with a more seasoned acolyte until I had learned the details. I loved it! I was moving with a purpose through this space, which had made such a deep impression on me and aroused my spiritual sensitivity. Two services were scheduled every Sunday—"the Eight" and "the

Ten." Before the ten o'clock service there was a lot of activity. Altar Guild members were cleaning the table from the eight o'clock service and resetting it for the late service. Choir members arrived one by one and robed in the room adjoining the sacristy. But the eight o'clock service had no such activity. It was the quiet service. There was only one acolyte. Soon I found my name on the schedule for my first eight a.m. service. This was my graduation prize! I was trained well enough to be trusted to carry the service by myself.

Full of excitement and anticipation, I rode my bike to the church and went into the sacristy. The rector had already vested in his full length, white, tailored alb. It had a high, starched collar, embroidered with a red cross at the back. He had been waiting for my arrival. As I put on my red cassock and white surplice, he opened the wide, deep drawer marked with the word "White" and unfolded the poncho-like vestment with an opening in its center called a chasuble. In one sweeping motion he lifted it into the air, letting it settle over his head and onto his shoulders. It was made of special silk, hand sewn with light blue velvet embroidered designs and matching blue taffeta lining. He looked splendid in this apparel. It denoted his unique place in the drama that would follow at the altar.

Each of us was tending to the task of getting ready. Then he approached me. I was worried that I had gotten my vestment on backward or that it was not hanging properly on my shoulders. In acolyte training we had been taught to check each other for such things. I supposed that, since there were just the two of us, this was what he had in mind. He put one arm around my shoulders as if to straighten things out, but next, with his other hand, he lifted my face upward toward his. He stroked the back of my neck. Then he kissed me on the lips as he had the day I was sick. But this time, his mouth opened and his tongue searched my lips like a snake, probing and parting them so that he penetrated my mouth. I felt his hand on my waist, pulling me toward him.

Nobody had ever said anything about this part of the ritual. What was going on? What was I supposed to do? I couldn't breathe. My mind simply could not process this shocking new experience. This was a frighteningly different kiss, different from anything I had ever experienced. "You are so special to me," he said. "You must know how much I love you." I knew how much my parents loved me. This didn't feel like that. I could taste the sweet mint flavor of his tongue. I could smell the chasuble he was wearing, that peculiar aroma, the medley of the oak drawer, the myrrh incense, in clouds of which it was bathed at high services, the cotton shroud with which it was protected when laid out in the drawer. I could hear the tree branch scraping on the window. I could feel his hand on my chin, his arm at my waist, details embedded in my memory to this day. "Remember," he said, "this is our secret. No one must ever know what we do here!"

Then, everything changed. He straightened up. His face became hardened and serious, like a different person. It was as if nothing unusual had happened at all. He stepped back, reached to the desk nearby, and handed me the card from which we were to read the Preparation for Worship. I could hear the coughs and shuffling of the congregation gathered down in the nave beyond the heavy oak door, waiting for the sacred worship to begin. We stood face-to-face, the only distance between us the fourteen-inch length of the cards we held in our hands. We spoke in hushed voices. It felt like a secret rendezvous to which God was now politely invited.

THE PREPARATION (abbreviated)

Note: Make the sign of the cross where the text is marked with a (+).

Priest — (+) In the name of the Father, and of the Son, and of the Holy Ghost. Amen.

Priest — I will go unto the Altar of God.

Acolyte – Even unto the God of my joy and gladness.

Priest — (+) Our help is in the Name of the Lord.

Acolyte — Who hath made Heaven and Earth.

Priest — I confess to Almighty God, to blessed Mary ever Virgin, to blessed Michael the Archangel, to blessed John the Baptist, to the holy Apostles Peter and Paul, to all the Saints, *and to you, my brother*, that I have sinned exceedingly in thought, word, and deed, through my fault, my own fault, my own most grievous fault. Therefore I beg blessed Mary ever Virgin, blessed Michael the Archangel, blessed John the Baptist, the holy Apostles Peter and Paul, all the Saints, *and you, my brother*, to pray for me to the Lord our God.

Acolyte – May Almighty God have mercy upon thee, *forgive thee all thy sins*, and bring thee to everlasting life.

Priest – Amen.

Acolyte — I confess to Almighty God, to blessed Mary ever Virgin, to blessed Michael the Archangel, to blessed John the Baptist, to the holy Apostles Peter and Paul, to all the Saints, *and to you, Father*, that I have sinned exceedingly in thought, word, and deed, through my fault, my own fault, my own most grievous fault. Therefore I beg blessed Mary ever Virgin, blessed Michael the Archangel, blessed John the Baptist, the holy Apostles Peter and Paul, all the Saints, *and you, Father*, to pray for me to the Lord our God.

Priest — May Almighty God have mercy upon thee, forgive thee all thy sins, and bring thee to everlasting life.

Acolyte — Amen.

Priest — (+) May the Almighty and Merciful Lord grant unto us pardon, absolution, and remission of all our sins.

Acolyte — Amen.

We finished with the Lord's Prayer and the sign of the cross. I drew the lines in a cross over my heart, but what did they mean? Was I marking myself as "Christ's own forever" as I had been taught, or was I crossing out emotions I could not explain? I was having a hard time getting it all to make sense. Everything had happened so fast! No time to ask now; the clock had run out. He looked at his watch and nodded. I took a deep breath and opened the sacristy door, rattling the loose terra-cotta tiles at the threshold, and led him into the brightly lighted Chancel as the congregation rose to their feet for the beginning of the Eucharist. The hidden drama had ended, and the public drama had begun.

This happened a number of times over the years, each time progressing a little further in intimacy and with the commensurate reward of his increased approval. But the incongruity of the two rituals—his passionate and sensual behavior overlaid by the words of the Preparation left me in turmoil and confusion. Was I being good or was I being bad?

It was an important question. Every night of my young life I ended my prayers by asking God to "help me be a good boy tomorrow." As my mother turned down my light to leave, I would ask her, "Was I a good boy today?" Her answer was always yes, but now I was not so sure. There was a tug of war going on. Which was I? A particular moment in the Liturgy itself reassured me. Partway through the service, we performed a mini-ceremony called the Lavabo. I carried a small bowl in one hand, a cruet of water in the other, and a linen towel placed over one arm to the corner of the altar. There he washed his hands under the water as I poured it. Standing close, I could hear him whispering the words from which "Lavabo" takes its name; "I wash my hands *in innocency,* O Lord; and so shall I come unto thine altar" (Psalm 26:6). I didn't quite know what "innocency" was, but I knew that when someone was innocent, it meant they hadn't done anything wrong.

A lot of what I needed in order to make sense of these things I did not yet have. Things were being done to me that I could never have explained then. I did not really know what we were "doing here." I was a child trying to take the words and actions I had to work with and make sense out of them. There was just a lot of my brain that had not come together yet, literally. I didn't have the equipment to be dealing with this stuff. The few times I ever had the courage to ask if it was right to be doing these things, he insisted that this was the way it was meant to be. "It is a higher way," he would say. "It is something men and boys do." He was the holy man. I was the child. I was too young to know that such feelings and pleasures were not appropriate with a man twenty-four years my elder. I did not know that being my priest did not give him the right to exploit me for his own pleasure with no thought whatever regarding what was happening to "my self, my soul, and body." In the Eucharist , he would say;

> ". . . and here we present unto thee *ourselves, our souls and bodies* to be a reasonable, holy, and living sacrifice unto thee; humbly beseeching thee that we and all others who shall be partakers of this Holy Communion, may *worthily* receive the most precious body and blood of thy Son Jesus Christ, be filled with thy heavenly benediction and made one body with him, that he may dwell in us and we in him." (Book of Common Prayer 1928)

As far as I could tell, we *must be* worthy and we *must be* one body with Jesus; and Jesus *was* dwelling in us and we *were* dwelling in him. We had beseeched God to make these things so. These words meant a lot to me. I took comfort in them. I took them literally. I did not yet realize that he was eviscerating their meaning. It would take many years for me to reclaim them, even as I recited them myself in behalf of my congregations as *their* priest.

I cannot say what sexual exploitation does in any other circumstance, but within the context of religious space and practice, it is distinguished by its utter schism of body from soul. In my own holy space, I sensed that something was not right, but since there was no category for this, I filed it deep within. I set it aside, wrapped it, and put it away. I had no label for it, because I could not understand what was taking place in that corner of my heart. Thus I laid up a depository of mistaken conclusions that tormented and misled me for a lifetime.

Helping Out

On several occasions the rector called our home to invite my older brother who was fifteen to go to the movies with him on Sunday afternoons. My brother demurred, even as my father encouraged him to go along. "After all," my father would say, "he doesn't have a family like we do. He's probably lonely. Why won't you go?" But my brother had heard and seen enough to know what this was about. He knew, but he never told. He was adamant in his refusal, and the solicitations ended for him.

One Sunday afternoon the call came to ask if *I* could come to the rectory to help with the mailing of the Diocesan magazine, of which he was the editor. I asked not to go. My father said, "Look, he needs help, and we help out when we are needed. Get ready; I will drive you over." We pulled out of our driveway onto Route One and drove about a mile before turning into the church compound at the farthest end from the rectory. We wound our way past the sacristy door, around the tower, and down the long drive to the rectory path. My face was hot. My hands were sweaty. My heart was racing. Time was running out! Refusal was not an option. I could not think of any way to tell my father what I knew was likely to be there to meet me. He slowed the car down, came to a stop, and told me to call home as soon as the rector was finished with me. I opened the door and slowly walked around the front of the car. Before I had walked ten feet up the fieldstone walk, I heard the car slip into gear and the crunch of ice and gravel under the tires. My father was gone.

It was a winter afternoon, and I could smell the wonderful aroma of the hardwood burning in the fireplace. I slowed my pace, watching my feet come into view—first left, then right, carrying me along to the place I did not want to go, as if they had a mind of their own, defying my will and making their way there in spite of me.

When I reached the door I stood for a moment, knowing that once I was inside, I would have no way to manage what was to come. I paused, considering that I might just turn around and walk home. But I knew that if I did, I would have to answer to my father. How could I possibly tell him the real reason that I did not want to come here? And what if "Father" had seen us arrive? He would call and say that I had gone missing and I would hear how disappointed he was that I had not come when asked. I stood there, feeling very small facing the large oak door.

Suddenly it opened, and we were face-to-face. He was wearing a beautiful silk robe and slippers. I knew then that I was right regarding what this afternoon was really going to be all about. He took my jacket and hat and laid them on the chair in the entry hall. I had thought we would be working in his study, the room with the many panes of glass that looked out on the front drive. However, he led me into the living room where the fire burned brightly in the fireplace. The drapes, which usually hung at either end of the broad expanse of glass, had been drawn. A long, narrow table had been set up in front of the sofa at the center of the room. On it were several piles of glossy covered booklets, the Northeast, the diocesan news magazine, which he so often edited while sitting in our living room. There were labels and stamps to be moistened with a damp sponge and applied to the magazines to prepare them for mailing. Crackers and cheese and cider were laid out on the sideboard. This was to be a pleasing afternoon for him, I could see that.

It began well enough. He instructed me in what I was to do, and we began. He tended the fire from time to time, prepared some crackers, and poured some cider. We ate together and just as I supposed we would begin our work again, he came and sat very close to me. He put his arm around me and drew me closer to him and began stroking my arms and legs. Then he kissed me and began to fondle me. I was about ten by then, and these behaviors succeeded in arousing me. I looked up from the sofa where we were sitting and I saw the face of the Madonna I had seen on the tour. Her eyes were on us—tender eyes, sad eyes. Soon he suggested that we go upstairs, and I went. We walked up to the upstairs landing and into his bedroom. On the bed was the plush blue eider down puff we had seen on the day of the open house. He slowly undressed me and beckoned for me to lie on the bed with him. He played with my genitals by mouth and stroked the rest of my body until I had an orgasm. He did not ask me to do anything to him or for him. He simply used me to satisfy his phallic fixation. I wonder what the little tour group would have thought if they knew *this* was what happened in the master bedroom of the house with the funny name.

The Shadow Knows

There were other such occasions. One, in particular, stands out, for it was a day when in a startling moment we were "found." On that afternoon, after what I now know was his foreplay, he led me up to his room again. Whenever this happened, I was both excited and intimidated all in one confused and dazing fugue. He disrobed and, as usual, methodically and sensually disrobed me. This time he instructed me to stand on the plush carpet of his bedroom where he could take his kneeling approach. It was very quiet, save for the sound of a soft wind outside the windows. I was facing the open bedroom door. He had his back to it.

I gradually became aware of a shadow, cast by the lowering sun as it fell onto the carpet. Slowly, the shadow crept toward his open door. Then quietly, tentatively, someone appeared. It was the housekeeper, Mary! She stood in the doorway, her tiny frame silhouetted against the brighter wall behind her. Mary was watching us! What would this mean? Would she turn us in? Would she call my father? Here was a tangled knot of feelings. I was relieved and frightened, all in the same moment. Mary cleared her throat, as if she were going to speak. But in a split second he kicked his foot out behind him and slammed the door in her face. He never missed a beat. He went on as if nothing had happened at all. He knew he had nothing to fear. Who knows what was said when the day was over and I had left? She had very little power or position with which to defend herself for this brave act or to defend me. Despite her menial position, Mary *was* a resident of the place. He could shut her out; he could shut her up, but he could not erase what she had seen.

So it happened that she became the only grownup who knew, the only one who had ever seemed to come to my rescue. Yet she was a stranger to me; I barely knew her. In my mind I have made something more of her, a figment of my imagination. She is too important in my life to be left behind as nobody. I care about her. I do not want her life to have been meaningless, as it seems so likely it was. She was his servant. What was it like to live in that house? What else had she seen? What was it like to be a divorced woman in 1939 as the Great Depression wore on, the year she came to the place?

I imagine she had very little to call her own. I imagine she had struggled to break away from an abusive husband. I imagine she had no children. I imagine she was pretty much powerless, frightened about what was to become of her. I try to imagine her enjoying the grounds, the birds, the finer moments of the rectory life—its society and warmth; life in the kitchen where she did her cooking and where I *did* find her baking as my father and I repaired faucets and worked on the copper water tank that stood like a sentinel behind the Queen Atlantic stove. I like to imagine that she had breakfast with me there once and we talked and she smiled and told me stories of when she was my age. In my mind I often see her kind face. I imagine her asking me to forgive her for never telling what she knew. I would try to get my confused mind around my fear in the bishop's office that she *might have told* on the one hand and on the other, my sadness that, knowing, she did not tell. I have always wondered what *did* become of her. I have invented a cousin to whom she was able to go with her few belongings as refuge while she reconstructed her life. I want her to have been happy and find employment and be important to someone. I want her to have survived the years of secrecy and disgust and turmoil of knowing the things that went on and being unable to do anything about them.

The narrative I invented helped me carry the secret I was bearing. At least there was someone else who knew the things he did and never dared to tell; I was not the only one. I will never forget her, the real Mary I barely knew and the Mary I have imagined and invented and wondered into being.

"I Will Always Be . . ."

At about this time, work began on the completion of the "west end" of the great tower. This end of the church had been left unfinished since the tower had been erected forty-five years before. Under the skilled guidance of the rector, money was raised to complete the building in 1948. The red-stone granite quarry in New Hampshire was reopened to mine the stone. Stonecutters and masons were brought from out of state to lend their art and skill to the work. As is common in the raising of funds for such a project, the greatest portion of support came from a few major benefactors. The rector was a master at courting the wealthy. The parish leaders were putty in his hands. It was he alone who brought together the real money to get the job done. He was brilliant in the art of manipulation. My family members were not the only ones who fell under his spell.

He knew it was important to encourage participation by the whole community. To bring this about, a plan was devised by which the total cost of the addition was divided by the estimated number of stones needed to complete it. Members were encouraged to make their gift according to the number of stones purchased. The cost per stone would be $10.00, nearly $100.00 in the currency of 2013. I was twelve years old and had several lawn mowing jobs. I was paid 75 cents an hour. After thirteen hours work, I had raised my $10.00. I sent it to the church to buy my stone. Somewhere in that building today my stone has its place. I suppose that, depending on its location, it could be holding up some critical weight of the whole structure. On the other hand, it might just be in a nondescript place where it does nothing more than keep out the cold drafts of winter, but my stone is there somewhere. I received a prompt reply from the rector on formal church stationery:

> *Dear Carl,*
>
> *Imagine my pride in finding your gift of a stone for our new building! There are many members who will be inspired by your hard work and devotion. You will be able to remember for*

the rest of your life, things that have been made
possible because you were a dedicated member of
our congregation. Please know of my deep affec-
tion for you. Remember, too,
   I will always be your Father.

He undoubtedly signed many letters with the title
"Father," but for me it was a term of endearment.
I took it literally, as I believe to this day I was
intended to take it. *"I will always be your Father"* was
written on that separate line. It carried with it the
whole weight of the special place I occupied in his
home and in his life *and* the special place he occupied in my home and my life. I kept that letter and
rediscovered it many years later. It was important
to me because I had pleased the man whom it had
become my desire to please. The timing could not
have been more auspicious for him.

The Pact

It happened that at this time things were changing
in my own father's relationship to me. He had been
a radioman in the navy during World War I. He
loved electronics and had a sophisticated multiband
radio by his bed. We would lie on his bed together
and listen to his favorites: Jack Benny, Fred Allen,
Fanny Bryce, Red Skelton, Amos and Andy. More

frightening were the times that he would turn to the shortwave band and tune to stations in Nazi Germany, on which we would listen to the terrifying ranting and raving of Adolf Hitler. We knew no German, but anyone who listened to Hitler's oratory could be frightened merely by the sound of his voice and the menacing emphasis of his syllables. I felt safe there beside my father, who I believed could protect me from any danger. I had also enjoyed the many times he took me with him to his office on Saturday mornings where I was allowed to pretend being a radio announcer on his wax cone dictaphone machine or play with the gelatin ditto machine. While I did not always enjoy being his helper on the projects he did at home and at church, I had learned many things from him about plumbing, wiring, wallpapering, gasoline engines, and other mechanical fascinations. On many afternoons he would invite me to ride with him on his business trips to nearby towns where he investigated workman's compensation claims. We would enjoy ice cream cones together or buy fresh-made bread to share when we returned home.

But in 1948 things began to change. He became more withdrawn. He did not invite me to ride with him. We no longer shared the radio time. He became super critical of my school projects.

I felt as if I could do nothing right in his eyes. I began to dread his homecoming.

My father was a complicated man. Like all of us, he carried in his inner self the little child he had been. That little child made a significant impact on who he was and what he did that so perplexed me. He was the youngest of three boys who constituted his family until a little girl was born. Her name was Emily, my aunt Emily, whom I never met. Yet I have come to know her over the years. Her large, oval photo portrait hung at the foot of the stairs in our house. It was hand-colored in pastels. In it, she stands in the typical pose of the formal pictures taken by professional photographers of the day. Her hair is a lovely gold, hanging in long curls on either side. Her dress is sky blue, and she stands by a chair on which her hand rests lightly. Through that portrait she was a companion in our household for all the years I was growing up. I passed her every morning and every evening.

I knew my father loved her very much, for he would often tell us stories about her winsome ways. She would ask him to play "school" with her. He was to sit in a chair in the living room and she would stand, pointer in hand, and proceed to teach him arithmetic or spelling. Then she would switch places and pretend that he was the teacher so that he could hear her recite her latest memorization. He lovingly reminisced about how she would run and play in the leaves in autumn and how she used to love to sing with him. He was her hero, and she was the apple of his eye. It was very clear from his wistful memories that she occupied a very important place in his heart all his life.

He was twelve and she was seven when she confided in him that she had a very bad pain in her side that she was sure would go away overnight. "I don't want Mommy to know. She will call a doctor, and I don't want a doctor." She pledged him to secrecy, and they made a pact that he would not tell anyone about it, no matter what. She prepared for bed and kissed him goodnight, as she did with everyone in the family each night of her little life. But the night brought something terrible to pass. A doctor *was* called, and by the time my father was wakened in the morning, she had died of a ruptured appendix. The loving secret shared by my father with his little sister had become a pact of death. He never shared the truth with anyone for many years. He, too, was keeping a secret that hurt beyond words. I suspect that he had not been able to tell until he was a grown man. His darkness was too heavy for him to bear.

Among the many songs he used to sing in his

concerts was one he had often sung for us at home. It was written by Eugene Field and set to music by Ethelbert Nevin. It was his favorite, and it always made me cry. On stage before his public, he sang it like the professional he had been trained to be, but at home he struggled with a choked voice and his own tears when he sang it for us.

Little Boy Blue by Eugene Field (1850-1895)
The little toy dog is covered with dust,
But sturdy and staunch he stands;
The little toy soldier is red with rust,
And his musket moulds in his hands.
Time was when the little toy dog was new,
And the soldier was passing fair;
And that was the time when our Little Boy Blue
Kissed them and put them there.

"Now don't you go till I come," he said,
"And don't you make any noise!"
So, toddling off to his trundle bed,
He dreamt of the pretty toys;
And, as he was dreaming, an angel song
Awakened our Little Boy Blue——
Oh! the years are many, the years are long,

But the little toy friends are true!

Aye, faithful to Little Boy Blue they stand,
Each in the same old place,
Awaiting the touch of a little hand,
The smile of a little face;
And they wonder, as waiting the long
years through
In the dust of that little chair,
What has become of our Little Boy Blue,
Since he kissed them and put them there.
(Public domain)

It is no wonder it touched him so deeply, in light of
that harsh reality he had to face daily for his whole
life. Imagine his grief over the "little *girl* blue"
that he lost; like the little toy dog and the little toy
soldier who remain standing faithful to their play-
mate, who has left them behind. In his tears lurked
the sad question, "What has become of my dear
little sister to whom I tried so hard to be true, even
unto death, tragically *her* death?"

He was twelve. I was twelve. He was the
youngest of three boys, and so was I. *And* I bore his
name complete—a little boy, aged twelve, named
Carl A. Russell. I believe I became the little boy
that he had come to loathe as the perpetrator of an

irreversible tragedy that never stopped tormenting him. It had to be worked out somehow, sometime, and it happened when I was twelve. The timing could not have been worse. "Father" became my refuge, where I was treasured, caressed, fondled, and told that I could become part of something greater, unique, a "higher way"; that there would be rewards that only he could give me; that one day I would be able to drive his impressive car, the pale green Chrysler New Yorker and enjoy other perks by association with this darling of the Foreside and hero of my household who would "always be my Father."

Tower Watch

The dehumidifier thrummed night and day in the tower. My father had instructed me to climb the tower stairs every week to check that the drain from the reservoir was not plugged. Overflowing water could damage the organ, and it would not do to have it raining in the nave where the congregation was seated on Sunday mornings. I did this every week, religiously. One afternoon, while I was in the organ chamber checking the reservoir, I heard the tower stairs begin their ringing. Someone was climbing them. I was pretty sure who that might be. There was no way out! By now, it had become familiar to me. The early reactions of palpitations and rapid breathing, the fright or flight responses of my primitive brain had all subsided. I had been conditioned by now. Later on when I studied psychology at college, I was introduced to the subject of learned helplessness. It was first discovered in animals and later applied to human behavior. When an animal (or a human) is repeatedly subjected to pain in a situation, which they are powerless to change, they eventually become inured to it and behave in a passive, compliant way.

So I listened to the ringing stairs, the scuffing of feet slowly climbing the tower, and waited resignedly. Shortly he appeared at the door. Here we were, ensconced in a remote and hidden part of the building, and no one else would know. It was a perfect opportunity, and he made the best of it. As I reflect on this episode, I think what risks he took! My father had a key. The sexton had a key. Suppose they had come to the place. Suppose the stairs began their ringing again, this time trapping us both. Of course, it didn't happen. He held his tryst with me and led me out of the loft, descending ahead of me to be the first one out the door. In those days, before the hustle and bustle of church life as we know it now, he was well protected from discovery. No one frequented the campus much during the week. It made things easy. At the supper table that night I reported, "I checked the tower today."

Camp Is Very Entertaining

"You have a scholarship," my mother exclaimed, as I returned from my lawn-mowing job "Father just called, and he has arranged for someone to pay for you to go to the junior high conference." This was good news. It meant that I could get out of a whole week of my job at the Foreside Estate where I worked, mowing the extensive lawns.

"Wow!" I said, "Does it pay for everything?"

"As far as I know," she said, "Do you want to go?"

"Yeah, I do."

I had listened to my brothers talk about the Diocesan Youth Conference. It was the subject of much enthusiasm. Now it would be my turn! We sewed name tags into all my clothes, bought some new sneakers, and found a Bible that I could take with me for the classes. My folks drove me up on the appointed Sunday afternoon and helped me find my cabin. We unpacked my stuff and soon they left. Immediately, for the first time in my life, I felt the churning, throbbing, aching, empty feeling of homesickness. I wandered out of my cabin to realize that there was no one there I knew—no school chums and no one else from our parish.

Then I spied the rector. He was here, too, the family friend! I was not alone after all, and at camp I knew I would be safe. He could never be alone with me. The clergy who made up the staff of the conference were a mixed lot. Some of them were delightful. One was a skilled storyteller who fascinated us with his stories as we sat around the campfire in the dark. Another was an amateur magician who entertained us on the porch where we gathered between afternoon sports and hikes. There was an excellent pianist who led us in hymn sings but also surprised us with his jazz and extemporaneous "piano bar" renditions.

Mornings were spent in classes where we were taught church doctrine and Bible stories. One class was spent preparing for making our "first confession." As the classes progressed, we were enjoined to make a full and complete telling of every sin we could dredge up. We were given a little book entitled *101 Sins for Confession*. Had we been unkind to our school friends? Had we been disobedient to those who had charge over us? Had we touched ourselves or anyone else in an "unclean manner"? Had we been "unchaste"? Had we eaten more than we ought? Had we ever told lies to our elders? Had we ever thought impure thoughts? The possibilities went on and on. We listened to all of this, knowing that at the end of the week we were going to have to meet some priest in the chapel with those opening words, "Bless me, Father, for I have sinned." Then we would read off our list ending with "... for these and all other sins which I cannot now remember, I ask God's forgiveness and your counsel."

"Is this a full and true confession?"

"Yes, Father."

Things were getting complicated. First of all, in the Congregational Church days, I had heard my parents complain about "those Catholics" who go to confession and then just go ahead and sin all over again during the week. I had been taught that "we don't go to confession," a good protestant position on the matter. More importantly, I had some heavy-duty stuff that they were telling me I had to tell somebody else. How could I do that? What would I say? I concluded that I would have to lie again, this time to a priest. How would that go over with God—the act of confession as a sin of deceit?

In the meantime, there were the evening bed checks. Each cabin had an older teen as a counselor. They were responsible for making sure we were all in bed by lights out. At the appointed time the lights were turned off. Soon one of the priests would come to the cabin to make sure everything was in order and to say an evening blessing. The first night the storyteller came. The second night was the magician. They each said a prayer and left. But there were two nights when the cabin was darker than usual for me. I made my way to my top bunk. The counselor quieted us down. The lights were turned out. In came the priest. By his voice I knew it was the rector. He said the prayer, but he didn't leave. He came to my bunk and silently slipped his hand under my covers and fondled me; that was all. Then I heard the spring on the screen door creak and the door quietly closed.

The next night was more surprising. The priest who came was one of the rector's friends, Father Fitz, who appeared with the rector's other clerical friend in photos sent to my parents from faraway places where the three of them travelled together on holiday. The prayer was said, but the door spring did not creak. Again, silently, a hand slipped under my covers, and I felt him holding my genitals. I was shocked. This priest had been told! How else would he know he could do this? I never remonstrated. I lay there with his hand on my genitals and never made a sound. I was awake all night *that* night until reveille came blaring over the loudspeaker hanging on the tree outside our door. I understood the episode with the rector; there was nothing new about that. His friend was another thing all together!

Here was a new sin to add to my list. Attention had been given during the week to the sin of "touching oneself in an unclean manner." Nobody had said anything about someone else touching *us*. I would have to confess that I had let a *stranger* do it, and another priest at that.

Finally, the day of confession arrived. Our names were written on a schedule beside a time, at which we were to show up at a tent set up to serve as a chapel. The sides of the tent had been rolled up to make an open, covered space. From time to time during the afternoon activities I could look from afar and see one of the priests in his cassock, a purple stole over his shoulders, sitting on a little stool. In Anglican practice, largely among high church congregations, confessions are made at the altar rail. The priest is seated on one side of the altar rail and the penitent kneels on the other. The two can actually speak to and see one another. There is no anonymity. As the afternoon hours passed, I saw several different clergy take their place. The appointed hour came. I went to my cabin, opened my suitcase, and retrieved my list, which I had fastidiously hidden to be sure no one else could ever see it. I walked slowly toward the tent, list in hand. You can guess who was seated on that stool. Of course, it was the rector. I felt a great surge of relief. There was no need to tell all this to *him*. He already knew. That was why he was there. I knelt on the kneeling cushion and said the prescribed words. "Bless me, Father, for I have sinned."

"May the Lord give you grace to make a full and truthful confession," he answered. My list was much shorter than it should have been, but it included my confession that I had let another priest touch me in an unclean manner. There was a long silence. He cleared his throat. "And what was this priest's name?" he asked.

"Father Fitz," I answered. Another long silence. Then he continued, "Have you made a full and complete confession?" I finished the few remaining sins. He could have finished it himself. I was then assigned my penance: say the 23rd Psalm, the Lord's Prayer, and the General Thanksgiving from the Book of Common Prayer. When I told my brother this story, he said, "I had to make my confession, too. It was raining heavily, and when I said, "Bless me, Father, for I have sinned," there was a spectacular bolt of lightning and crash of thunder. "That was my *Last Confession*," said my brother.

After the Ball

In a family who had just joined the congregation, he had unlimited time to coax and coach me and my parents to the behaviors he desired most. In fact, I believe I was a very lucky target. His fetish was with genitalia. That was his focal point. I was essentially a passive object for him. He did not require more of me than that. Except for one time. Again, it is incomprehensible that he had so gained the advantage of trust from my parents and such power over me that this could ever have happened. By now, I was probably about thirteen.

On a warm summer evening, my mother and father explained to me that we would be joining "Father" and his close friend, Gladys, on a theater night at a famous summer playhouse. They picked us up in his Chrysler New Yorker and drove us about an hour to the theater where we saw a play, which was full of suggestive sexual content. I am not able to remember the name of the play, but I remember that the theme was the trial of two young people who had been found *in flagrante delicto* in a barn. The turning point of the play has them on stage in a courtroom where a Puritan Divine is trying them for moral turpitude. One line burned itself into my memory, especially in light of what would take place later that evening. Facing the audience and pointing an accusing finger toward the cowering couple, the Divine shouts, "They have pleasured themselves. They have *pleasured them-*

selves!' I remember my parents' anxious laughter
and the rector's boisterous enjoyment. When the
play ended, we were driven to our house, which
was located about a mile north of the church
complex. When we stopped, as my parents were
alighting from the car and I was expecting to leave
with them, he said to them, "I'd like Carl's company
to take Gladys home." To my dismay, my father
replied, "Yes, of course." The rector added, "I'll
drop him off on my way home." It was late enough
to be very dark, even in this summer month. He
invited me to sit in the front seat between him and
his friend.

Gladys was a spinster living alone in a small
bungalow nestled well back from the road, with a long,
winding drive lined with mature high bush rhododen-
drons and sumacs. I was familiar with the yard. I had
often mowed her lawn and trimmed her bushes. He
had introduced me to the job. When we arrived, as if
by prior plan, she quickly got out of the car, said good
night, went into her cottage, and promptly turned out
the light. He drove about half-way out of the yard,
stopped, and turned off the engine. This was a very
different situation from all the others. There was an
intense ambiance of intimacy. I did not know exactly
what was coming, but I felt anxious and vulnerable
in a way I had not experienced before. The interior

of the car created a muffled silence and privacy. The windows were open, and a warm breeze carried the aroma of nearby blossoms in the garden. The green velour seats were smooth and cool. I could hear the sounds of little creatures rustling through the underbrush. He drew me close and began to kiss me. Then he took my hand and placed it on his crotch. He had an erection, which seemed huge. He encouraged me to unzip his pants. I began to do it. He took a handkerchief out of his breast pocket. At that time I had no idea what that would be for. I did not know about ejaculation. He moved my hand up and down his genitals, encouraging me to caress them as he had done to me. Suddenly my whole body froze. I began to hyperventilate, and I had what I now believe to have been an anxiety attack. I took my hand away and said, "I don't want to do this." Nothing more was said. He zipped up his pants, put the handkerchief away, and tried to calm me down. I think he was frightened by my reaction. He said, "Be sure you don't tell anyone about this. People won't understand. It could be very bad for you and me if you do."

This had been the worst episode yet. I was shaking inside and out. I could not get out of my mind the huge erection I had been coaxed to touch and the feeling of danger that swept over me. I was tiny, by comparison. "Insignificant," is what I thought. "I am tiny." I have carried that impression all my life. And the velour seats, the velour seats; I could *feel* the velour seats, green there in the darkness. He drove the mile back to my house very slowly. Then, looking across the seat to where I was crouched against the passenger door, he said, "I want you to be with *me* when you come the first time." Come where? Come for what? Come when? I had no idea what he was talking about. I was so confused. Nothing about this whole evening made sense. How could I figure *anything* out when I was having trouble even catching my breath?

I was still short of breath when he dropped me off at the end of our front walk. My heart was palpitating, pounding in my chest. Every muscle in my body was failing me as I slowly made my way up the walk. I forced a swallow to see if I could take control of my breathing. I had the length of that front walk to extinguish the fire of my emotions.

The screen door at the front of the house was open and the light spilled out onto the steps from the sun porch. When I entered the house, my mother was folding clothes at the dining room table. She looked up from her work with a smile and said, "Well, didn't we have a good time tonight?" Had *they* had a good time? Really? What about the play? What about the language? What about the time that had passed since we left to take Gladys home? "Yeah, it was great," I said grudgingly and in disbelief. She didn't have a clue.

Mr. God

The Episcopal Church has its roots in the Church of England from which it parted during the American Revolution. In fact, its constitution was framed by the same men who were laboring to form the new government in America. While its political and ecclesiastical allegiances were changed, the fundamentals of its teachings still lay in the sixteenth-century adaptations of the Elizabethan Settlement. The issue of these parliamentary actions brought about a merging of both Reformation and Catholic theology. From then on, the church carried within its broad margins leanings to either Protestant or Catholic teaching and practice. In America these poles were referred to as "high church" (holding that it is only through the church that salvation is possible) or "low church" (holding that the church plays an attenuated role in matters of salvation). The rector vigorously held to "high church" teaching. As a result, the confirmation training we received made a strong case for the Sacramental Principle; that is, that things pertaining to the spirit were conveyed by tangible and visible means. The definition of a sacrament is "an outward and visible sign of an inward and spiritual transaction." So the outward and visible sign of water conveys the inward and spiritual action of God in the washing and cleansing of Baptism, by which people are grafted into the body of Christ. Likewise, in the outward and visible act of breaking and sharing common bread and drinking common wine, an inward and spiritual communion is effected by which we receive the body and blood of Christ.

As part of this training, we were taught about the sacramental mystery in the power of a priest to make present the person of God, the "priest as sacrament." To nonbelievers these things have little or no consequence, but when they are taught as tenets of family belief, that this is how it works, that this is "real," it determines how we behave, how we understand our world and what is happening in it. According to this understanding, the rector, as priest, made God present at the bedside of my dying Nana. He made God present to my grieving mother. He made God present when I was frightened by my delirium. He made God present in the sacrament of bread and wine in the holy spaces. A child cannot tell the difference. So a child surmises that if "he" is there in the bedroom, there on the sofa, there in the sacristy, there in the darkened car, God is present, and the situation is safe and approved, even if his gut is telling him otherwise. In legal terms this is called "fiduciary confidence." The role being played places the priest in the position of unmitigated trust. It is not earned by signs of integrity and competence, but *ex officio,* by virtue of the "office." Because of the position he holds, he is given the benefit of any doubt. The church has certified him as trustworthy, laid hands upon him publicly, and licensed him to occupy the role of shepherd. At the time, this belief was held in such high regard by everyone in my society that it was unchallengeable.

Look Around You

The power of this one man, who slipped into our life with such cunning and finesse, is hard to explain. As I grew older and my life took another direction, that power persisted. Even when he was no longer in our lives, the fear governed me. My mother and father died without ever knowing what had transpired. I had been asked in subtle ways, but I never told. Why? The language of context was what impressed me as the conveyor of the truth that matters. It is what I *saw* and *heard* around me of which I took note, not what was said in so many words.

My mother once sat down beside me on my bed and gently asked, "Is anyone bothering you, dear? You can tell me. It's all right." Those were the *words* that were spoken, but what were words next to the special treatment, the photo on the precious table, the power to grant permission regarding what we ate, the spotlight on the pulpit, my father's fascination with the clothes he wore, the garments in which he vested, the purple piping, the titles. All of these screamed in my soul, drowning out my mother's gentle voice. *They will never listen to me if I say anything about him. If I tell the truth, it will be my word against his and he will win.* The rector had made sure I knew. "If you ever tell, no one will believe you. It will bring terrible harm to me. It will be terrible for you. Don't forget that!" That trumped everybody and everything else. There would be no telling aloud!

Body Language

By now, the stress of my inner turmoil began to take command. Since there was no telling *aloud*, my body had its own way of telling in *silence*. I began a behavior, which I could not have explained at the time. Nor did anyone ever mention it or attempt to uncover the mystery that prompted it. It was effectively ignored by all.

It was at the family evening meal that our unity and identity were expressed. I had always loved mealtimes as we shared my mother's baked beans, clover leaf rolls, and coleslaw with hot dogs. Or, during the war years of rationing, when each of us had our own little portion of sugar or butter or meat. Table talk was lengthy and inclusive. There were anecdotes, recounting of favorite family lore, much laughter and sharing of ideas. When we were gathered like that, there was a deep sense of belonging. But by the time I was fourteen, that changed. Little by little I began to feel like an outsider. I was carrying a cumbersome secret. My self-talk was saying, "If they really knew, they wouldn't love you. You don't belong here." I was caught between the interior secret, which I could never tell aloud, and the consequence of keeping that secret—alienation from my family. The temptation to tell was excruciating.

Eventually, I began to act out in a bazaar way. It only happened when my body was telling me I needed a bowel movement. Without excusing myself I would get up from the table and go hide behind a door that opened onto an adjoining room. From there I could peer through the narrow opening on the hinged side of the door and watch my family at the table. I would do this while crossing my legs to hold back the moving of my bowel. After an interval of this, when my bowel had settled down, I would return to take my place at the table.

When I discussed this with my therapist many years later, we talked about how literature and the Bible speak of the bowel as the center of emotion and sensitivity. Since the bowel is designed as a place of containment, in vulgar parlance our language expresses keeping to ourselves what is really going on inside us as "holding back our shit." My body was doing just that. I had a lot to hold back.

Good Grooming

As a grown man dealing with these memories, I cannot imagine why I cooperated so willingly. When I think about my brothers' ability to refuse him, I wonder why I did not. Not only that, but I had begun to think that something about *me* was what caused him to desire this. I began to blame *myself* for my predicament. Somehow, *I* was seducing *him*. What *was* it about my genitals that lured him in this way? They had become a cause of terrible anxiety. I wanted them gone. Sometimes when I was alone in the family bathtub, I would experiment by stretching my scrotum up over my penis and wonder how I could sew it in place to cover this shameful and troublesome part of my body, to seal it from him once and for all.

In much of the therapy I have done over the years, I have had to be helped to understand the methodical process by which, beginning at age seven, I was slowly conditioned to accept this behavior as something appropriate for me to participate in. It is called "grooming," and it is a definable part of the strategy of a pedophile. Here is an explanation posted on the Internet by the program *America's Most Wanted*. What a difference it would have made then to have this sort of information so readily available to my parents! There was no Oprah Winfrey to bring these things into public view as she has so often done, no documentaries on *America's Most Wanted*, no Dr. Drew to explore the lives of those involved. This was socially proscribed information. The resulting silence protected the predator and left the innocent to fend for themselves.

> The statistics are startling. One in five girls and one in ten boys are sexually exploited by adults before they turn eighteen. Perhaps the most startling fact is that most of the time the victims know and trust the adults who abuse them. So

where does this trust come from? Pedophiles tend to be very patient and manipulative. They use four basic tactics, called "the four F's": Friendship, Fantasy, Fear, and Force. The adult will usually give the child gifts, take them on special outings, and show them a lot of attention.

Friendship And Fantasy

"Friendship" is built with a technique pedophiles use called "grooming." Grooming a child is nurturing a friendship through bonding. The adult will usually give the child gifts, take them on special outings, and show them a lot of attention. Once a child trusts an adult, the adult can influence the child's attitude regarding sexual behavior. Grooming may include introducing sexual content to the child as an example of what the perpetrator desires and to give the impression that the depicted acts are acceptable. If the child thinks that sex between children and adults is ok, it's easier for the pedophile to victimize the child. Then the pedophile will introduce "Fantasy." They will manipulate the child with a false sense

of security. They will pay a lot of attention to the child's problems and personal
matters and offer advice and counseling.
They will tell the child how much they
love them and that they want to have a
long term, loving relationship with them.

Fear And Force

Once the child has opened up to the
pedophile, they will begin to instill "Fear"
by threatening to share the child's secrets
with their classmates or their parents.
Sometimes the pedophile will even
threaten the life or safety of the child
or of their family and friends. It's all a
manipulation tactic to get the child to do
what the pedophile wants them to do.
Ultimately, the pedophile uses "Force" to
sexually exploit the child.[1]

The process is deliberate and opportunistic. The
rector had found the perfect candidates for realizing his fantasy—a family mesmerized by his
style, indebted to him for his ministry, investing
unwarranted but freely proffered trust, beyond any

---

1   Source: *America's Most Wanted* http://www.amw.com/features/fea-
ture_story_detail.cfm?id=730

doubt. Carefully he had tested the waters with my brothers and, while they had rebuffed his advances, he knew that they had not revealed anything that they knew. He had skillfully groomed my parents, as well. He had blinded them. Now he was drawing the boundaries of his safe space. He could be bold and brazen with the seven-year-old he had begun with. I was swept neatly into his web, and the more I thought to get out, the more I knew I was locked in. I slowly became disintegrated—flesh from spirit, body from soul. It is as if he literally sucked the heart out of me through that place on my body. No wonder I began to hate that part of me! In spite of his proffers of love for me and the times he talked about my special place in his life and affection, it was my penis he desired, not my self. Being a child, I did not know the difference, but the shame of it drove a wedge into my person and pried the parts one from the other.

Something More

By the time I was fourteen, my situation had become so uncomfortable that I could no longer cooperate with him. There was more to my life now than the narrow world that had surrounded me, the world of infatuation with this man. There were other important people in my life now—teachers whom I admired, my scout leaders. These all had an impact on my thinking. I was reading literature and history and glimpsing another whole world. I was developing internal desires I had never had before. I had made friends at school and visited them in their homes where the rector meant nothing to anybody. I was developing a stronger sense of my self, as well as maturing physically. I was beginning to realize that my body was my own and I had the right to decide whose I would be. I began to object to his behavior and refuse him.

When I returned to high school in 1951, my sophomore year, having just turned fifteen, my life was changed in a heartbeat. It was morning band practice. A girl carrying a clarinet case entered the rehearsal room, a new girl. She was stunningly beautiful, and I fell in love with her instantly. She was handing out music, and when she came to my place, I could barely speak. For weeks after that I followed her, asked others about her, and set my heart upon her. I was responding to the mere sight of her with my body, as well as my mind and my spirit. For the first time in my life, I experienced lust. I saw her in my dreams and wrote poetry to her. I had never felt anything like this. I finally mustered the courage to ask her to eat lunch with me. Eventually, we were "going steady," and I could not believe that someone this beautiful would actually want me to be her boyfriend. Our relationship has lasted now for sixty years.

I made a point of telling him about the girl I had met and that I thought I was in love with her. I had very little contact with him thereafter. He knew his fantasy was finished, but he did not give up easily. Within days my father asked to talk with me. He sat me down and said, "I have had a talk with Father, and he tells me that Greta's family is part of an odd church group. He does not think that she is a fit girl for you to date." I knew right away what was happening. In a last ditch appeal to my parents' allegiance and fears, he was aligning them with himself in a campaign to discredit the girl I now loved and to lead them to forbid my courtship. I determined, then and there, that he would not prevail. For once, I stood up to my father. I told him that I intended to continue my relationship with her. I believe that if he had persisted in trying to obstruct my love for her, I might well have resolved to tell the truth and take my chances on my word against the rector's.

The only sanity in my inner life now was my relationship with the girl I had fallen in love with. She was a lifeline, a reassuring sign that there was another way of life for me. I clung to her for dear life. In our attic are two boxes of letters. One is the size of a child's shoebox. The other is a full-sized briefcase. In the briefcase is the collection of my love letters to my wife. I wrote one every day that we were apart. By contrast, all of the letters she wrote in return are comfortably contained by the shoebox. These are testimony to the almost pathological dependency I had on her to reassure me that my affection was appropriately placed. I continued to court her. I met her family. Eventually, they learned of my church affiliation. Her brother was ten years older than she was. He and his wife took us to the movies one evening very early in our relationship, before either of us could drive. As he drove us home, he said, "Well, your pastor has quite a reputation!"

I said, "What do you mean?"

"He likes little boys," he said.

"Oh really?" I pretended. My ears were red hot, and my heart was beating hard and fast. I was stunned. I was incredulous.

"Oh yeah," he continued, "one of my friends took me to that house when we needed money. He disappeared for twenty minutes while I had milk and cookies with the housekeeper. When he came back, he had the money, and we took off for the store."

I stammered my way through the rest of the

conversation and ended it as quickly as I could manage. *Was he on to me? How much did he know? What could he tell me about me? And this, in front of my new girlfriend!* Not only that, but this was the first time I had heard that there were others involved. I had always thought I was the only object of his attentions. It was a shock!

Many months later I passed my driver's test and was issued my license. One afternoon when we were alone together in my 1936 Dodge coupe, she finally asked me what he had meant. Was I ever involved? On that one occasion, I told her that he had tried to touch me but only once and that I had refused. I kept these secrets from my own wife for decades, unable to muster the courage to tell her the whole truth. I lived in terrible dread that one day her brother would tell her something that would implicate me and I would lose her forever. Here began the process by which I would bury this story deep in my inner man, in denial and regret that would last for three decades before erupting and demanding my attention once more.

Chapter Three

Moving On 1954 – 1961

Close Encounter

In the summer of 1957, at the end of my junior year in college, I was sent to London, England, by a very wealthy woman for whom I worked summers. There, I worked as a Winant Volunteer in the East End. The East End had been heavily bombed by the Nazis. Twelve years after the end of World War II, reconstruction was still under way. It was not just that buildings needed restoration, but the people themselves were eager to connect with people who would reach out to them. My assignment was to work with families under the auspices of a church in the Isle of Dogs across the Thames from Greenwich Palace.

One afternoon I received a phone call. "Hello, Carl. This is 'Father.' I'm here in London on holiday. How would you like to join me for lunch?" An explosion of emotions and memories ricocheted across my brain. How had he learned of my whereabouts? My parents! He was still writing them regularly. They must have told him. Perhaps they had even suggested this. What was this about? I was a long way from home. My fiancée was not with me. I was alone in a devastated part of the city. Here was someone "from home."

By now I was getting a hold on my racing thoughts. During the time between his disappearance and now, I had a lot of questions to ask him. I was old enough to know that his behavior with me was outrageous. I had thought many times how I might challenge him if I ever had the chance. Now was my chance. This was an opportunity to tell him how I felt about what he had done. If, in his mind, it was a rendezvous, it was to be a moment of truth for me.

I said, "Sure. Where shall we meet?" The place was near Piccadilly Circus, a fine restaurant, fitting to his tastes. As I entered the dining room, I spied him at a table near the window. He was well dressed, but he did not appear as I had ever seen him before—no black suit, no clerical collar. He stood to shake my hand. "How good to see you again," he said.

Who is he remembering? I wondered to myself. There was so much that he had missed in the years that had passed, since he had rolled up his window and driven away, leaving me standing by the mailbox. I was engaged to be married in a year. I had nearly completed my college education. I had matured sexually; I was a full-fledged man, not the child he had so easily seduced and manipulated. Whatever he knew of me, he had learned from his continuing correspondence with my kindhearted mother. It was possible that he had no other interest than to catch up on my life, to let my parents know that he had contacted me in this faraway place that he knew so well.

Though I was then about to turn twenty-one years old, the effect of being in his presence was to stir up all the old fears. How was he going to make his move? How would I deflect it? We ordered. The conversation took the usual course of catching up. He had received his doctorate. He was a professor at a major university in New York. He was responsible for student affairs. *Ah, I thought, you are well placed! What happened to the therapy you were supposed to have? What about the chaplain's supervision? You've got them all fooled. Nothing has changed.* As we were waiting for our meal, I decided this was it. "You know," I said, "the things you did with me were wrong. Why would you do that to a kid?"

Smiling and throwing back his head ever so slightly, he replied, "I was only trying to give you the chance to follow a more rewarding way. There is a whole world out there that I could have shared with you. In fact, I was wondering if you would like to come and meet some friends of mine here in town." No remorse. No apology. He was going on as if I had said nothing. He brushed my feelings aside as he always had. It was still all about him. He had actually planned to take me and show me off to his friends. I declined, but as I look back on that moment, I realize he still had me in thrall. The combination of fear and shock silenced me. Why did I not stand up, then and there, and walk out of the restaurant? Why? That is what this book is about. Instead I fled to the safety of pleasantries. He advised me on my travel plans. We finished our meal and parted. I never saw him again, except in dreams and nightmares, and the word pictures I drew for numerous therapists as I tried to sort out the craziness of it all.

Take Thou Authority

Having completed my seminary degree in 1961, I was ordained deacon in the Diocesan Cathedral. Six months later I was ordained priest. Though I was serving in a small mission congregation that would have been thrilled to have an ordination take place in their own space, their claim was preempted by my sponsoring parish, the place of the conspiracy of my childhood. Why did I not insist upon being ordained in the congregation where I now belonged? Yet, on December 21, 1961, the Feast of St. Thomas, the Apostle, I was ordained priest at the scene of my abuse.

Ordinations in the Episcopal Church are a little like mini-coronations. After all, the Head of the Church of England is the monarch who is crowned by the Archbishop of Canterbury. The theological premise in both cases is that something particular is conferred, something that implies an endowment with godly powers and preferment. I was to receive the same imprimatur and certifications that the rector had. I had spent four years in college and three years in seminary to prepare for this moment. That gave me plenty of time to consider the implications of what I was doing. I cared *about* the church, but I hated what had happened to me *in* the church. Fortunately a new rector had guided me through the process of preparation. He was a robust, loving, married man who had just finished a tour of duty as a chaplain in the Korean War. He was seasoned, well adjusted, and did much to repair the damage done to my idea of being a priest.

In "The Ordering of Priests" in the 1928 Prayer Book, there is a point at which the people of the congregation are seated. The bishop sits in the center of the chancel at the head of the aisle and calls the candidate to be brought forward from the congregation. With grave and dignified emphasis he delivers the church's charge in the words quoted below. They are the very words delivered to the rector at his own ordination. I have italicized the words that have particular significance to me.

> Have always therefore printed in your memory, how great a treasure is committed to your charge. For they are *the sheep of Christ*, which he bought with his death, and for whom he shed his blood. The Church and Congregation, whom you must serve, is his Spouse and his Body. And if it shall happen that the same Church, *or any Member thereof, do take any hurt or hindrance by reason of your negligence, ye know the greatness of the fault, and also the horrible punishment that will ensue* . . . Forasmuch then as your Office is both of so great excellency, and of so great difficulty, ye see with how great care and study ye ought to apply yourself, as well to show yourself dutiful and thankful unto that Lord, who hath placed you in so high a dignity; as also to beware that *neither you yourself offend, nor be occasion that others offend.*

The bishop then laid his hands on my head, the traditional sign for the conferring of the Holy Spirit. By custom, all of the clergy present gathered around me, placing their hands over the bishop's hands. I could feel the weight of them, as if to emphasize the weight of the office itself. Then he said the coveted words:

> Take thou Authority to execute the Office of a Priest in the Church of God, now committed to thee by the Imposition of our hands. And be thou a faithful Dispenser of the Word of God and of the Holy Sacraments. In the Name of the Father and of the Son and of the Holy Ghost. Amen.

Next, I was to be vested in the Eucharistic vestments as a sign of my authority to celebrate the Holy Communion. The chasuble, the poncho-like outer garment, had been carefully taken from the wide storage drawer marked "White" and laid out by the Altar Guild. It was the very one worn by the rector sixteen years before in his first erotic advance. In silence, the clergy appointed lifted the chasuble to place it over my head. As the garment fell over me, I was enveloped in darkness. The commotion was silenced, as if I had crawled into a snow cave. I felt like I was suffocating.

Chapter Four

Things Seen and Unseen 1961 – 1984

The Invisible Dog

When I was little, I opened my stocking one Christmas morning to find two little plastic Scotty dogs, one black and one white. Each was attached to a small, square magnet. On a table top, with a little care, you could make one move by bringing the other slowly toward it. As you did so, you would feel a little resistance. Slowly you crept up from behind until the other little dog began to move. The chase was on! But if you approached too quickly, the other dog would snap around and grab you. It was a wonderful experiment, showing the invisible power of magnets to attract or repel each other. Another trick was to place one dog on the visible side of a thin sheet of cardboard. The other dog was placed underneath so that by magnetic attraction the visible dog could be made to appear as if it were moving of its own volition. Here was an example of how one dog could govern the behavior of the other. I have thought of these tricks on many occasions when, in spite of appearances, my life has been driven by powerful forces hidden beneath the surface, the secrets that hurt me and others around me.

I have been left with a number of peculiar idio-syncrasies, which seem to be related to my child-hood experiences. Several examples come to mind. One evening my wife came home with a video of the movie *Pavilion of Women*. She had planned a cozy evening together by the fire, sharing some hot chocolate and watching the film. As the movie unfolded, it came to a scene in which an older man is forcing a young girl to commit fellatio. She is resisting and crying and pleading to be released. As the scene began, it was clear what was coming. I became anxious and hostile. Suddenly, I jumped up, letting my wife, who had been leaning against my shoulder, fall back against the sofa. "I'm going to bed," I shouted and stormed out of the room. I was out of the room before I realized what I was doing. I went to the bedroom and sat on the edge of our bed. I remained there, determined not to go back to the living room.

In a few minutes I heard my wife slowly climbing the stairs. The door was open and I heard her whisper, "Are you OK?" I was holding my head in my hands and I silently gestured no. She came to sit down beside me. "Why would you bring that movie home and blindside me with it?" I growled. She sat there patiently, holding my hand.

Gradually, I got hold of myself. "I don't understand why that upset me so much," I cried. "What is wrong with me?"

"Let's just fast-forward through that part and watch the rest together," she suggested. Fast-forward! What a great solution. It worked. We had our evening back. If only it were possible to just fast-forward through *all* the detritus that is left behind by sexual abuse. But fast-forwarding our embedded memories just doesn't work that way.

One Christmas, my wife excitedly carried her gift from our tree and laid it on my lap. As she looked on expectantly, I opened the box and lifted out a beautiful silk robe. With barely a thought, I immediately folded it and put it back in the box. I then proceeded to scold her in front of our children for spending so much money on my gift. I told her I hadn't asked for a bathrobe and I would never wear a bathrobe. "Besides, I hate silk," I said. She was crestfallen. She had *given* me a gift; I had *received* a very bad memory. When I saw the silk robe, I was seeing the rector, standing at the door, waiting for my arrival on that cold and cozy winter afternoon. She put the box aside and we went on with the exchange of gifts. Inside I was feeling terrible. I knew I had hurt her, but I could not tell why. Later, I apologized for my behavior and accepted the gift. It hung in my dressing room for years and I never wore it. Occasionally my wife would wear it, but I resented that very much. I have no idea where that robe is now, but it would not be welcome, even if I did.

I have never had any close friendships with men. To this day, I will not join men's groups. I do not care to spend time alone with any man. I never played athletics. I will not enter a men's locker room, and when I use a men's toilet, I always go to a stall because I am ashamed to be seen.

I dislike bare feet. When I see bare feet, I see *his* bare feet. I simply cannot participate in the ceremonial foot washing on Maundy Thursdays, as the Book of Common Prayer prescribes. The idea of letting someone else handle my feet or for me to handle another's seems sensuous and dangerous. When I officiated at Maundy Thursday services, I provided an alternative *hand* washing for people like me.

Having been a priest for my entire career, I have had what I call a "love-hate" relationship with the church. The little boy who was so much affected by the beauty of that first Sunday in the new church and saw firsthand the effect of a caring ministry could love the church that made that possible. But the little boy, who had been over-powered and exploited and misguided, distrusted the bearers of power in that same church. My ordination resulted from a contest between a genuine calling and the driving passion to be in charge so that nothing like my abuse could happen to me, or anyone else for that matter. If the rector were in a position to overpower me, I would *become* the rector. After all, it was when others had control that I could not be safe.

For example, early in my ministry I had the opportunity to oversee the building of a new church building. As I met with architects and builders I became adamant that every office door, every church schoolroom, and especially the sacristy should have expansive windows, giving transparency to anything that took place within. In every congregation that I served, I felt compelled to make the same arrangements. In this way I dealt with my obsession to make certain that the holy spaces were safe spaces. I was fixated on transparency. This was puzzling and amusing to many of those with whom I worked, but in due time the issue became more widely acknowledged.

As the scourge of sexual abuse within the church became widely known and publicized, many churches, in order to show "due diligence," required what they called Safe Church Training. In the Episcopal Church, every bishop was required to verify that anyone working with children in a church setting had taken this course. This was largely driven by fear of litigation. It was not until heavy financial losses were being incurred that care was taken. While many were conscientious about taking these precautions, the idea that the issue can be resolved by education seems to me to be beside the point. When the diocese in which I was serving required the clergy to sign a document certifying that they had never, in their entire career since ordination, had any dealings with parishioners involving inappropriate sexual relations, I signed it and wrote a note of protest, saying that it was naïve to think that anyone who had been deceitful enough to be involved would have any scruples about signing such a document. As it turned out, some bishops who required this due diligence and attested to it were found to have been offenders themselves.

These are just a few examples. In spite of my many years of work, they still plague me. One thing I have learned from my struggle with this truth, lying hidden in my inner man for so many years, is this: putting the pieces together and finally making some sense of what happened does not make the pieces go away. They remain to be contended with, one by one, in a struggle to get free from the impediments they place in our path to living freely. Childhood sexual abuse is trauma. Often, as in my case, it can last many years. Such trauma, experienced repeatedly over years, lays down pathways in the brain that become hardwired. The primitive brain records that certain situations are dangerous. These "triggers" are like emotional landmines buried beneath the terrain which, when stumbled upon, ignite a charge far greater than the issue of the moment. They cause a "fight, flight, or freeze" reaction, which is not subject to rational assessment until *after* we have "acted out." By then it is often too late to retreat. My experiences with the rector had planted many such mines. Uncontrolled outbursts and unexplained hang-ups that I have spent a lifetime trying to explain now make sense as I reflect on the things that happened to me in my childhood. These are the consequences of the invisible dog of truth that lurked in the recesses of my brain.*

For the Bible Tells Me So. Really?

Most of my reactions were benign and harmless, involving windows and doors and my own inhibitions and outbursts. They did not involve harm to

---

*For more on this, see *The Developing Mind* by Daniel J. Siegel, MD, Guilford Press. Available through Amazon.com ISBN 978-1-57230-740-7 (pbk).

other people, except for my family. However, the most dangerous seed that germinated within me was my fear and suspicion of homosexual people. I had managed to achieve my goal of ordination. I had become the rector who had the power of the pulpit and the influence given me as a teacher. These were the very shields I had determined to carry as my defense. I became proficient in the knowledge of scripture, and I often wielded it as authority to support my prejudice. To me, *all* homosexual people were predators. I had never even considered that there could be any difference between a pedophile and a homosexual. In order to protect myself from the greater truth of what had happened to me, I had mistakenly connected homosexuality and pedophilia. The facts show that pedophilia is more prevalent among straight men than in gay men and that few gay men are pedophiles. This is the power of our personal experience, or our fear of it, as it informs our ideas and drives our behaviors. It is reinforced by a culture of prejudice, which, sadly, currently prevails in our land. For three quarters of my career I was a leader of those who sought the methodical elimination of any rights or opportunities for gay people. My suspicion of them was palpable.

In 1976 I was a Deputy to the General Convention of the Episcopal Church. This meant I was elected by my diocese to cast my vote in matters of church life. In preparation for this, my bishop asked that I attend a meeting at the Episcopal Divinity School in Cambridge, MA, where Deputies to Convention would be able to meet a group of gay people who had agreed to become vulnerable and openly discuss their lives and issues with us. I became very angry and told the bishop that I would have nothing to do with this attempt on his part to *influence* the votes of Deputies and to *desensitize* us to the "gay agenda." I took myself to the convention that year unspoiled by any rational consideration whatever. As at most such events, there were large meeting rooms that adjoined a very spacious exhibition hall. As I looked about that hall, I came upon one of the exhibits sponsored by Integrity, the organization of gay Episcopalians. I was almost paralyzed. I could not look them in the eye. I could not converse with them. I resented their presence and, more importantly, I feared them, though I did not even know them. Some of them were fellow clergy.

It was at this convention that the church finally took an official action voting that homosexual people are children of God. The resolution reads as follows:

"*Resolved*, the House of Bishops concurring,

That it is the sense of this General Convention that homosexual persons are children of God who have a full and equal claim with all other persons upon the love, acceptance, and pastoral concern and care of the church." As I write this I can barely believe that such a resolution would even be necessary, but at that time I had my doubts. Noises were being made, even then, about gay people being allowed to be ordained. It was not even a formal resolution. I became apoplectic.

I have the text of a sermon I preached upon my return, in which I announced that if an openly gay person were ordained to the priesthood, I would be forced to resign my Holy Orders. I was bent on protecting the church from anything that could replicate what had happened to me. If Holy Orders were compromised in this way, then how could it continue to work for me as my means for coping with the priest who molested me? Little did I know that my own child, who sang in the children's choir, sat at the foot of the pulpit, and listened to my opinionated ranting at home was struggling with issues of sexuality and gender himself. Without knowing it, I created a hostile world for him that nearly drove him to suicide. And into the bargain, I laid a foundation for the same fears and prejudices in my whole family. So much for using my influence to create "safe space!"

Several years after I had left the state where
all this had happened, I was nominated as a candidate for election as their next bishop. It was down
to four other candidates and me. As part of the
interviewing process, we were asked to explain
what issues we would address, if elected. Among
several sensible and informed suggestions I made,
I felt compelled to announce that the first thing
I would do was to identify all homosexual clergy
and remove them—a witch hunt followed by some
means of purgation. After all, this would be the
ultimate opportunity to create the safe church I
had not enjoyed. I expostulated from the scrip-
tures in support of this strong stand. At the election I received the lowest number of votes by a
wide margin. As I presented myself then, I would
not vote for me, either. That is how the little dog
I could *not* see was directing the little dog I *thought*
I knew.

Yet there was an unseen exception to the hardened attitudes that I held publicly. One of the men
in my congregation came to tell me that he was gay
and that he had just been diagnosed with HIV/
AIDS, at that time a pronouncement of certain
death. He was a prominent financial adviser in our
town, the chairman of our Finance Committee

and rightly admired by many. His condition was so dire and he was so fragile that, in this moment, my pastoral instincts outwieghed my fears. As he became more and more ill, I spent time with him in the hospital. He was deeply devoted to the church. When I went to visit, he had selected hymns to sing together and prayers that he wanted me to say. He carefully planned communion services for me to celebrate at his bedside. These moments were very moving for me. Eventually he was unable to move or speak. He was at home, and his lover was caring for him with deep affection and failing energy. He, too, was afflicted. Finally, Ernie died. I buried him, and I tended his forlorn lover until his own death.

In my personal, pastoral relationships with homosexual people, I was not governed by the fear that drove me in my public pulpit persona. There, I was energized and persistent. I preached a sermon, which I titled "Truth and Consequences," in which I argued the prevailing mood of the day that somehow those who were suffering from AIDS were reaping the harvest of the seeds they had sown. I expostulated on the few but oft-quoted passages in the Bible that seemed to condemn homosexual acts.

Unfortunately, I was a convincing preacher, and I did great harm in arming the wrong people with a message they could use to hurt others around them. I deeply regret those years. They were the years in which I was keeping secrets that hurt not only myself, but also many others. Considering these things from a new point of view, I realize how easily Holy Writings can be abused to support prejudices that derive from other sources. Holy Writings are far more like soft clay than hard stone. They can be shaped by the unexamined attitudes we bring to them. As long as my heart was hardened toward homosexual people, I was able, by selective editing and strict construction, to argue my case. The discourse in my mind was founded on the premise that all homosexual people are perverse and predatory. The question with which I began was, "How can I prove that they are bad?" Without any consideration of what might be lodged in my mind driving my prejudices and convictions, never searching myself, I came to conclusions that were ill-conceived and sabotaged my own proclivity toward love and caring for others.

Friends in High Places . . .
Because I was a member of the Standing Committee of the diocese in which all of this had taken place, I was present when the new bishop presented a petition for reinstatement to Holy Orders. The

signature was familiar. It was the rector himself. The bishop, who apparently hadn't looked into the facts of the matter, spoke in favor of this request, which would officially reinstate the rector to be a priest in good standing in the church. I was astonished that it had all come back into focus. I was also in a quandary. I could not support it, but I was unable to muster courage to tell the truth about my involvement that I would need to support my opposition. The chancellor of the diocese was an *ex officio* member of the Standing Committee. He was the only other person in the room who would remember the facts. He had been present at the meeting with the county attorney in the bishop's office with my father when it was agreed that there would be no prosecution if the rector were deposed. He knew all of this, but he also knew that he was constrained by the agreement from revealing any of the details.

However, there *was* something that *was* common knowledge. It was the campaign that had been waged by the rector to discredit the previous bishop who deposed him. The diocese had sought to raise a fund in gratitude for that bishop's twenty-five years of ministry as the leader of the diocese. Envelopes were printed and sent to all Episcopalians in the diocese in this form:

*My gift in thanksgiving
for the 25th anniversary of
the ministry of the Rt. Rever-
end Oliver L. Loring as Bishop of Maine.*

My family and many others in the diocese had received duplicates of this envelope on which all of the lines had been blacked out save for the last, thus reading, *"end Oliver L. Loring as Bishop of Maine."* They had been carefully prepared and mailed by the rector. On the basis of this, the chancellor argued that to vote for reinstatement while the former bishop was still alive would be an insult. I was saved from having to speak against it and thereby having to reveal my own secrets. The argument prevailed, and reinstatement was denied. But it was never put to rest.

I had been away from the diocese some years when I received a call from the President of the Standing Committee of that diocese. He called to tell me that *another* petition for reinstatement had been received from the rector, and the committee would be acting on it that morning. He asked if I knew of any reason why it ought not to be approved. My throat tightened. I broke into a sweat. I closed my eyes as I sat at my desk and entertained the anger that was creeping over me. How could this be considered yet another time? The man just would not give up! He must have known that the chancellor had died and I had left the diocese. Had anybody checked the files of deposition at the Diocesan Office, the file marked "For the Bishop's Eyes Only"? Didn't anybody care about the young men who had been seduced by him, who had carried their own burden, as I had, for thirty years? I knew that the man calling me at that moment cared. He had been in a position to guess at my involvement with the rector. He was giving me the chance to be heard. The opportunity to prevent reinstatement was at hand, but I could not summon the truth, even then. Instead, I resorted to the argument from ten years before, severely weakened by three decades of faded memory. "He remains unrepentant for the damage he did to our former bishop," I argued feebly. What my inner man was shouting was, "What about the things he did to me and the others he damaged? Has he ever said he is sorry? Can anyone certify that he has been rehabilitated?" My complaint was never heard. I said nothing. In spite of my anger at the county attorney, the chancellor, the bishop, the senior warden, and my own father for their deliberate avoidance of charging him with his crimes, I had not made progress enough to intervene when I could. The committee voted to reinstate him. He was returned to active ministry with all of its prerogatives for the rest of his life.

Chapter Five

From the Deep 1984 – 2008

Eruption

In 1980, in southern Washington State, volcano watchers were keeping watch on Mount St. Helens, which had a long history of extensive quiet times with intermittent periods of volcanic activity. For 120 years, until the early spring of that year, the mountain had been a bucolic backdrop of beautiful forests, mountain streams, lakes, and fresh air. Hundreds of families had built their homes nearby. But in March the hidden powerful forces operating deep beneath the surface began to reveal themselves in measurable ways. Minor tremors were felt. Then a noticeable swelling occurred on the side of the nine-thousand-foot mountain. By April, signs of the tremendous forces churning deep within were undeniable. On May 18th, in a horrendous explosion of gasses, white-hot lava, mudslides, and ashes blown miles high into the atmosphere, the top of the mountain blew off.

In 1984, with aftershocks of that disaster still vivid in the public mind, I experienced my own eruption. The secrets that I kept buried had a life of their own, fermenting in the darkness of my unconscious self. Despite the warnings of many smaller flare-ups over the years, I had built my own emotional home tenuously on the slopes of a mountain of memories and fears. They were about to erupt and compel me to come to terms with the truth one way or another. It happened in my kitchen while I was peeling potatoes. It was my turn to prepare supper for the family as my wife was returning from Boston on the commuter train. The radio was set on National Public Radio as usual when I was working in the kitchen. I took a moment to enjoy the view from the kitchen window, looking past the oak tree at our son's horse, lazily grazing in the field below. "All Things Considered" was playing as I fumbled with the potatoes, wet and slippery in my hand. My mind was enjoying the idea of this rare evening at home, free of any responsibilities. I barely noticed as the program moved on, but my reverie was disturbed by a word here and a word there, like sleet against a windowpane; "priest" – "children" – "cover-up." Unbeckoned ideas were nudging their way into this placid moment. I lost track of what I was doing and where I was. My mind did not want to join the conversation, which was insisting itself upon me from the radio, but it was irresistible. I was listening to breaking news of a scandalous cover-up by the Archdiocese of Boston involving the sexual abuse of dozens of children by undisciplined priests.

Water boiled vigorously on the stove, ready for the potatoes I had been cutting up. I could feel myself becoming agitated by what I was hearing. All those children! I imagined I heard a child weeping. The work in my hands became blurred. I was blinking my eyes to wash away tears. The weeping child held my attention. I don't remember how long I stood there crying, leaning on my arms against the cold sink. I was slowly summoned from this trance by commotion in the adjoining room. My wife had arrived. Our son was greeting her in muffled conversation. I was barely aware of her approach. Then I felt her arm on my shoulder and her warm kiss on my neck, drawing me back to the moment. "What's going on?" she asked. I turned to her and saw a look of uncertainty and tentative alarm. I wanted to explain to her what had happened, but I hardly knew what it was myself. There were emotions and images I recognized as familiar but did not want to own as mine. How could I share them with her? I shook my head without speaking.

She took my hand and guided me down the echoing hall and into the quiet of the carpeted living room. We sat together on the sofa for quite some time before she asked again. What was troubling me? I wiped the tears from my eyes with my fist. We both knew that something, still nameless, was about to be unmasked. I was able to tell her that there was much more to my story than what she knew; there were things I had not managed to tell her for all our years together. As I spoke, I felt our whole life was about to change, one way or another. What would she think of someone she trusted to have no secrets, who had kept so much from her? This was the moment I had dreaded from long ago when her brother had grazed the truth in the conversation in his car. I looked straight into her eyes. Would she shake her head in disgust? I wouldn't blame her.

Without hesitation, she took me in her arms and held me. "Go ahead," she said. "Go ahead and cry. I know it's going to be OK. We'll get through this." Some old feelings were creeping in—fear and shame vying to displace my overwhelming sense of relief and gratitude. Somebody who loved me was staying right here with me, no matter what. The lie of silence had ended. Over the next days things kept making their way to the surface. In a momentary excursion, my subconscious had revealed more than I had ever previously been able

to face. But there was a great deal more to be reckoned with. Like an iceberg, what had been revealed
was only the peak. It would take many more years
to discover the whole that lay buried beneath.

Inner Healing

Over the years that followed, I became involved
in Christian healing ministries, working out my
own "stuff" without realizing it. As part of this,
I attended a week-long healing conference in
Rutland, Vermont. The leaders were Francis and
Judith MacNutt. Francis had been a Roman Catholic priest in the Dominican Order, the preaching
order of the Roman Catholic Church. Judith was
a skilled psychologist. They are widely recognized
and respected as wise and balanced teachers of
spiritual healing. Together they have taught and
written about it, beginning with one classic written
by Francis simply titled *Healing.*

At the conference, my wife and I had been
asked to be one of several prayer teams stationed
around the room, which held about three hundred
people. Our assignment was to be alert to anyone
who might show signs of sorrow or even agitation
and go to them to offer support and consolation.
Francis had completed one of his excellent teachings on the healing of memories. "Now," he said,

"I would like you to close your eyes and be quiet." Books were closed, chairs were shifted, and the room settled. "Now imagine yourself in a place where something painful has happened to you. Imagine that place in some detail. Where are the windows? Where is the door? What color is the wall?" There was a long pause. "Now imagine the thing that is troubling you in this place. Be quiet. Take your time. Get the picture in your mind and in your heart. Now I am going to sing quietly, and I ask you to imagine Jesus entering that space. Observe him carefully. Where is he coming from? How does he enter? Now give him a little time. What is he doing? Record in your mind what he is doing and put your trust in him. Let his Spirit control the situation you are in."

Then, in his tremulous voice, he began to sing without words. I had my head up and my eyes wide open, as the prayer teams had been instructed to do, but my mind was full of pride. I thought to myself, "I know all this. I've done this before." I was surprised by my detached and cynical attitude. However, we had agreed to be part of this. I would watch for someone who had been overcome with tears or agitated and we would go to comfort them. But it didn't happen that way.

All at once, I saw in my mind's eye, a little boy

standing in a green bedroom. His back was toward me and a man was kneeling in front of him, just as I had experienced when I was a child. It was the very moment Mary had seen so many years ago. Someone entered in a halo of light from behind my shoulder, passed by me, and went to stand behind the little boy facing the kneeling man. He gently lifted the little boy in his arms and set him aside. Then, to my astonishment, he took the little boy's place. Without hearing any voice, Jesus's declaration echoed in my thoughts, "In as much as you have done it to one of these my little ones, you have done it to me."

I felt no overwhelming emotion at this vision. I did not cry. It simply became a new fact in my memory. It is something I can relate to you as if it had actually happened. In many ways it surely did "happen" to me. It is, by far, a better memory than the ones lodged in my mind for so many years. Here was the answer to my prayers for recovery. I decided to let it replace the memory it had so clearly "healed" in me. I began to speak of it to others, and I experienced a large measure of peace. This was it. My long nightmare was over. I had finally experienced the healing of that memory. I have come to learn, however, that while we may envision something wonderful, the inner realities require more. There are no "quick fixes." The vision was a promise, a guarantee of something more to come. For me, that made the hard work of therapy and recovery worth doing, but it was a long time coming. I lived on the strength of the vision for a decade, going about my business and my life, but I was not dealing with the disintegration that continued to hobble me in my profession and in my personal life.

Regrets

By the time I reached retirement, the professional costs didn't matter any more. I was no longer dealing with bishops or vestries or parishioners. Whatever the influence for good and ill, those days were over. What remained was the life of my family. I began to see the ways I had been attentive to the church family, while ignoring the importance of forging a family in my own household. The parish saw me at my best, and my family saw me at my worst. Admittedly, it was more complex than that, but my family *did* have to hear my ranting and complaining about church leaders with whom I contended. They heard my hyperbole about gays. They competed for attentions *they* deserved, while I gave preferment to everybody else who laid claim to me.

My ambition to hold power gave the church unwarranted influence in my life. By never saying "no" to anything asked of me in the church, I shortchanged their life at home. I could easily justify my behavior; it is what I had been taught in seminary—God first, the church second, my wife and children third. In a church descended from the Roman Catholic practice of celebacy, marriage was still treated as a concession. During my years at seminary, my wife was not even permitted to worship in the Chapel with me. She was required to remain behind the ornate carved screen and participate as best she could during the Chapel services. One of my bishops, visiting in our living room, once said, "Well, Carl, we have to acknowledge that in some ways we are *bigamists*. We have taken vows to our wives and vows to the church." My wife quickly retorted, "No, Bishop, I think you are *adulterers*. The church is *Christ's* bride, not yours!"

Of course, many of my family memories are pleasant ones, but there are also many regrets. As my wife and I reflected on our lives, we seemed to be dwelling a lot on the things we had either misunderstood or about which we had made decisions that were harmful to each of our children and to all of them as a whole. Our youngest son observed our sadness and spent a lot of time reflecting on these things with us. "What is the use of standing still in your sadness?" he said. "All of us (siblings) have been hurt, but you can't change the things that happened then. What you *can* change is how you relate to us and to each other now. You won't change the family until you change yourselves. You would probably get a lot of help by talking it out with somebody. Why not go see Michael?"

Michael was an acquaintance I had known many years before. I respected his unique way of seeing the world. He was a free spirit, a wonderful blend of innovation, wisdom, joyfulness, and compassion—a lot like the one whose name he displayed on his license plate, "Friar Tuck." He was now a full-time therapist. Having been an Episcopal priest himself, he brought a compassionate understanding of the ways that dysfunction in the church system impacts the lives of the members of clergy families. That is where we began, but somehow it seemed too obvious, too simplistic. After a few sessions, Michael sat back in his big chair and said to me, "I think we are beating around the bush. There isn't going to be much progress in the family until you deal with the things that happened to you as a child." That is how my work began in earnest.

Roots

In the yard of our house, there is a modest tree. When we moved in, it was weak and stunted by a vigorous growth of bittersweet. This voracious vine, which cannot create a stable structure of its own, was clinging and wrapping itself around every branch of the tree and threatened to quench it. Yet to the eye, at a distance, the whole appeared to be rich and verdant. My wife and I spent several weekends sorting out the one from the other. We could have simply snipped the vines at their base and let them wither, but that wouldn't have kept them from returning. We needed to search out the roots and unearth them. We needed to get our hands dirty. Each single tentacle had to be painstakingly unwrapped and cut away until the counterfeit growth was cleared and the integrity of the little tree was recovered. Then the roots had to be dug out. This is the best metaphor I know for the kind of work I had ahead of me. To get to the authentic Carl, I had to deal with the snarled places and unwind the tangled strands from the healthy growth. What was needed was a kind of emotional and psychological horticulture. It was time to get my hands dirty. It took awhile, a long while. Eventually, in a memorable session, when the timing was just right, Michael introduced a new character to my story, one who would help me come face-to-face—with *myself.*

Me and My Teddy Bear

Across from me on my desk sits a small, brown teddy bear. He is 18" from head to toe with a black button nose and two alert beady eyes. His ears are cocked forward as if to listen attentively, inviting conversation with whoever might be inclined to speak to him.

I was having some hard going as Michael worked with me on the stubborn grasp of shame. As I resisted his gentle nudging toward the idea that perhaps I was not really the one to blame, he got up from his chair, walked behind a wicker room divider, rummaged around a basket, and came out carrying the teddy bear. He placed the bear on my knee so that we were face-to-face. "Meet Little Carl," he said. "Take your time. Look him in the eye. Get to know him. See if there is anything you'd like to say to him?"

My wife was sitting beside me, as she usually did in my sessions. We all sat in silence. I became very aware of the drone of the air conditioner. I looked at the beady eyes and the cocked ears and the tight little mouth. No one broke the silence. The little bear seemed to me to be very vulnerable. His eyes seemed to be asking something of me. I stammered, "This is really strange. What am I supposed to do here?"

"Is there anything you would like to say to Little Carl?" Michael asked, softly.

"Well, I guess I'd like to tell him that he is making me feel sad right now," I said.

"Don't talk to *me*," said Michael. "Talk to *him*." My wife reached over and gently took my hand in hers. I shuffled in my seat. I held the teddy bear in my hands and lifted him off my knee. I put my face near his face and thought hard. What did I want to say to the little boy I had been talking *about* for so long? This was the first realization I had had in all my life that I could talk *to* him.

All those years between then and now were like a time warp. I was face-to-face with the little boy who had so much shame and confusion. Then, from deep inside, from that reservoir of my past, an irresistible sob worked its way through all the sandbagging I had so laboriously laid up over years of denial. I whispered to the teddy bear, "I am so sorry. I am so sorry!"

Michael prompted me again, "What are you sorry about? Tell him what you are sorry about."

"I am so sorry this happened to us," I cried. "I am so sorry you had to go through this." I was surprised by what I said next. Looking him in the eye, I said quietly, "I am so sorry I did not protect you from him, but I was so small. I couldn't do anything about it. Do you understand me? Can you forgive me?" Silence.

I knew the session had come to an end. My time was up. I looked at my therapist and said, "Wow!" He said nothing in return. I looked at the teddy bear again and handed it back to him. I knew we would discuss this at my next session.

Then he said, "Take him with you—everywhere!"

"Well, but I am taking my wife to dinner on the way home."

"That will be just fine," he said. "He can go with you."

"You mean, into the restaurant?" I said anxiously.

"Everywhere!" he said.

I became agitated. "What will I tell people?"

"Well, introduce them."

"But I have to lead worship and preach next Sunday."

"That's great. Take him to church. Carry him down the aisle. Let him sit with you. That would be a very good thing to do."

We walked to the door. I turned and said, "See you in a week."

"Everywhere!" His last word.

As we made our way to the elevator, I handed

the teddy bear to my wife. After all, people might understand if she were carrying it. Perhaps she had purchased it for a grandchild. She looked puzzled and said, "I don't think you get it." The elevator door opened upon a gaggle of people. I nodded, sheepishly holding my little friend under one arm. They smiled. I knew what they were thinking. "Look at the old man. Probably dementia. Probably headed for the nursing home." When we reached the car, I decided to seat him in the console between the seats. By lifting the console cover, I created a little back against which he could sit. When we arrived at the restaurant, as I unlatched my seat belt and opened the car door, my wife said, "You *are* taking him with us, aren't you?" We were seated in a booth. I placed the teddy bear on the bench beside me. She said, "Come on; get him up where people can see him." I placed him against the wall amid the salt and pepper shakers and the sugar packets.

When the waitress came to light the candle, which was precisely in front of him, she said, "Oh, isn't he cute. Whose is he?"

"Mine," I said reluctantly. "Well, in fact he is supposed to be *me* when I was little. It's a long story." She winked and said, "Will he be ordering this evening?"

A few days later, it was time for my dog and me to make our usual visit to the hardware store. This would be the acid test. Would I have the courage to show up there with my teddy bear tagging along? I assumed my most confident air and walked up to the counter. The two clerks who have prided themselves on their lighthearted and well-meant insults stood transfixed at the sight. "Don't ask," I said. "Sooner or later, I will get around to explaining all this." They smiled knowingly at one another and left it at that. It was a kindness I will not forget. And so it was, as I faithfully carried him with me from place to place. It was amazing how readily people cooperated in my assignment.

Holding Hands with God

My wife and I had been filling in at a local church while they searched for a new pastor. Since it was my turn to take the service, she had planned to be out of town with a friend. I would be leading worship alone. Well, not exactly alone. I was beginning to get it. The time had come for me to let my shame-filled child meet my world. I had successfully shut him out for sixty years. While I had tried to keep the church a safe place for others, I had never believed it could ever be safe for him. I had prepared my sermon before the therapy session

I have described. The title was to be "Holding Hands with God."

It was based on the first two verses of Psalm 40.

> I waited patiently for the Lord; he turned to me and heard my cry. He lifted me (*by the hand*) out of the slimy pit, out of the mud and mire; he set my feet on a rock and gave me a firm place to stand. He put a new song in my mouth, a hymn of praise to our God.

I had a fitful Saturday night. Over and over, I cast in my mind how I could explain the teddy bear. How would I get him in there? Where would he sit? What would people think? Would it be safe for me to tell the truth? On Sunday morning I put the teddy bear in his place beside me and drove to the church. As I walked from the car, I spied one of the children outside the entrance clutching his own teddy bear in his arms. *This is uncanny*, I thought. I went over to the little boy and said, "Hi Jerry. You've brought your teddy bear to church, too, just like me. What is his name?"

"Drew," he answered.

"Hello, Drew," I said. "This is Little Carl." We compared teddy bears for a few moments, and then I told him that "Little Carl" and I had to go get ready for church. I said, "Will you bring your teddy bear into church so mine won't be alone?" He smiled and looked at his mother. She nodded.

There was no formal entrance procession. When the prelude began, I entered quietly, carrying the teddy bear, and took my place. I held the teddy bear on my lap. The children took a particular interest in this novelty. I looked at Jerry and he smiled. I had decided that I would simply hold the teddy bear's hand through the first part of the service. I took him with me to the pulpit when it was time to deliver the sermon. Holding his hand in mine, I began.

Do you remember one of the very first Beatles songs? "I Wanna Hold Your Hand"—number 1 on charts in 1964.

I began singing the song. The people smiled, and some hummed along with me. I continued:

Holding hands is a significant human expression. It is not something we take lightly. Holding hands can mean a lot of things—all of them important and all of them signifying relationship. Holding hands in a circle is perhaps the most casual. But for those of us who do it, perhaps for prayer, sometimes to sing a song, sometimes to say grace, whatever it may be, it is an expression of unity and fellowship. When we greet each other, we hold out our hands and take one another's hands as a gesture of peace and agreement, that somehow we are bonded.

This verse from Psalm 40, which we have said together, brings into our mind's eye some very powerful images. I am thinking of the picture I saw on C-SPAN of a terrible mudslide in Brazil where nothing but an arm was reaching from under a wall of mud, a hand searching for another hand that could rescue and save. I watched transfixed as a rescue worker—those angels of mercy that appear wherever disaster strikes—reached for the hand and pulled the living person out from the mire.

And what about the images of the rubble at ground zero on 9/11? Holding hands may mean someone has come to our aid and we are being rescued and "given a firm place to stand on." People held hands for consolation, encouragement, and sometimes to reassure a trapped victim that another human being knew their plight.

Holding hands can be very deep expressions of devotion and intimacy. Let me share three such moments from my own life. I will never forget the first time my wife let me hold her hand. We were only teenagers. I was transported by joy. The language of that moment was truly beyond words. It said, "She cares about ME!" I felt empowered—that feeling that I could do anything! Remember *My Fair Lady*?

I sang a little of, "I have often walked down this street before," from *My Fair Lady*.

Or the time when our daughter was a little girl holding my hand in a crowded mall at Christmas time, in the midst of a throng of people. How proud I felt and how very critical I knew it was that if she lost hold of my hand she could be lost. Guess what? I lost her hand and I lost *her!* I could hear her cries, "Daddy! Daddy!" My yelling, "Where are you? Where are you?" The fright of that! We were both frightened. What a critical point of contact—her hand in mine!

On the evening my father died, my mother stood next to him, holding his hand. Tears made their way down her cheek, falling to the sheet beside him. She squeezed his hand intermittently. What was communicated in those final moments? Tenderness. Consolation. A life of loving. How important hands were when there was so little else to help them connect and time was running out!

I paused and waited for a few seconds.

Now, I ask you to imagine holding hands with God. Take a minute.

God is always offering us his hand for all the reasons I've mentioned and many more. According to one sensitive translation of another Psalm (63), there is a beautiful picture formed in the mind of the one who first sang: "My soul clings to you, your right hand holds me." These psalms are love songs. They are a pouring out of a heart which is filled with love for God, sung by someone who not only has a hunger for God, but who has come to that wonder-filled moment of understanding that God loves him so much! It is not only the moment for knowing that, but the transformed life that follows, when our hearts (our souls) are beating in a new rhythm that comes from a whole new idea of who we are as we bathe in the love of that Someone who has taken us by the hand. And imagine the joy in God's own heart when he feels our hand taking his—in the mall of this mad world in which we are planted.

Much of the Bible is about the love affair between God and humankind. Some of it is like a love letter from God; that's really what Gospel means—good news—God loves you, like this. Over and over God speaks to us in terms of endearment. This

is perhaps the most important feature of
our faith; our understanding of God is
built upon the promise and testimony of
so many that God is personal and deeply
desires to be on intimate terms with us;
that God is singing, "I wanna hold your
hand."

That first time when my wife let me
hold her hand and squeezed—her first
intimate signal that I was loved in this
new way—has been very important to
me over and over again. Not merely at
the human level, which I treasure, but
more importantly, by her gift of love, I
began to know what it means that God
loves me like this. That God takes me by
the hand like she did, and by taking my
hand, connects my heart and soul with
God's own. Like the one who sang these
psalms, my soul can cling to God and
my hand can clutch God's hand in the
terrifying places where I am out of my
element, where to lose my hold on God
would mean being utterly lost, that when
I come to this altar Sunday after Sunday
and take the bread into my hand and

touch the wine with my lips, an eternal connection is expressed there.

As I approached the closing of the sermon, my heart began to race and my mouth became very dry. I was speaking the words I had prepared, but in my mind an argument raged. *Go ahead and do it. But what if they are offended? Take a chance; trust them. They're singing with you. It is time to tell the truth.* I looked at the people. They were attentive, but I was about to put my life and my healing into their hands. Each one who had come today was, from my point of view, appointed to be "the church" which had never been safe for "little Carl." He was here with me today, and I could either leave them wondering what on earth I was doing with a teddy bear in church, or I could explain it all and take my chances. I mentally put my hand in God's hand and, holding hands with the teddy bear, I went on.

As you can see, I have brought a teddy bear to church this morning. You may have thought it was for the children's sermon, but since Marie has already done a fine job with that, you can see it is not. Let me introduce you to "Little Carl." I am working very hard with a therapist to

come to terms with the shame I have felt
all my life since my family's priest abused
me as a child. For many years I have
brought my grown-up self to church. As
a grown-up, I knew I could keep myself
safe there. But I never brought my little
self to church. Church has always been
unsafe for him. I have managed to get
myself pretty much cut in two, and it is
time for me to get my act together. That
is why I am holding hands with this little
guy this morning.

By this time, a number of people were weeping.
Something had touched them, but I could not tell
exactly what. What I *did* know was that I had found
a safe place. I went on to finish what I had prepared.

At the time of my death, I hope that people
dear to me will be at my side, holding my
hand as I complete my journey. And I
expect that somehow, deep in my spirit,
I will be able to hold God's hand, like a
child, and trust God to lead me on to the
safe place that has been prepared for me.

I stood there with the teddy bear and said nothing

more for a whole minute. There was almost complete silence except for the clearing of throats and the muffled sound of the children in their church school rooms. Some people sat with their eyes closed. Others had their eyes on the teddy bear. I was reluctant to break the silence as I announced the hymn, "Precious Lord, Hold My Hand."

During the hymn I walked to the altar, where I would celebrate communion, and placed the teddy bear there. We went on with the service. When we were finished, I left on the final hymn and went to take my place at the door. The response was remarkable. Some people skipped *my* outstretched hand and gently shook hands with the teddy bear. Others took him out of my arms and hugged him. Others spoke to him and told him he was loved. Jerry's teddy bear gave my teddy bear a "high five." It was a morning of healing.

Reflecting on Michael's wisdom in giving me the teddy bear, I realize that I had never held a conversation with the child who had been abused. Instead, I had carefully encapsulated him in what I believed to be a "safety zone," while I went on trying to ensure that the church would be a safe space for others. This congregation had shown me that church *could* be a safe space for the whole of me. I had begun my process of reintegration.

A Very Pleasant Interlude

The following weekend, my teenage granddaughter borrowed my teddy bear to keep her company for the night during her sleepover at our house. In the morning at breakfast she said, "Grandpa, look at what I found last night." Opening a tiny, hidden zipper in the back of the teddy bear, she said, "Look." She reached in and brought out a tiny, shaggy, teddy bear from a pocket sewn into the soft furry back. She held it up and said, "Surprise!" I *was* surprised. All the places I had taken that teddy bear, I had no idea there was more to him than what met the eye. This was, indeed, a "find." Of course, I wondered what it meant. My therapist used the teddy bear to help me connect with "Little Carl." Here, in my hand, was something more than that. My heart? My psyche? My soul? The unseen self, the more-than-meets-the-eye in all of us? Whatever it stands for, I now think of the teddy bear differently. I see him in a new way. Whenever I look at him sitting on my bureau, I see "more" than I did before. I don't know how many more years I have to live, but there will always be something more to be found, the hidden part of me to work on, to grow and tend, for as long as I live.

Just Say No

Like most children, when I was small, saying no to an adult was an infraction of family rules. I learned *that* at an early age. As time moved on, my consistent exposure to sexual and emotional manipulation pretty much extinguished the very part of me I would have needed most to muster the courage to say "NO." Therefore, in every negotiated transaction of which I have been a part, I have begun with the premise that I cannot hope to prevail. In instances where I might have known how I could prevail, something inside me regarded my options as too risky. To eliminate the anxiety, I elected to abdicate my position or avoid the situation all together. This has been an impediment for me in various tasks ranging from overseeing staff to buying a new car.

On several occasions, my oldest son asked me why I seemed to have so much trouble with confrontation. Why would I not contest an error on a bill or demand that a journeyman complete what he had promised to do? Why would I not send a poorly cooked steak back to the kitchen? After one such conversation, he sent me a book that had been helpful to him titled *How To Argue and Win Every Time*, by Gerry Spence. In the book, the well-known attorney, writer, and television host writes:

What is power? The power peculiar to
each of us is that force that distinguishes
each of us from all other beings. Our
power permits us to grow and to fulfill
our potential. It is the surf, the swell, the
wave, the storm we feel in our veins that
propels us into action. It is our creativity.
It is our joy, our sorrow, our anger, our
pain. This energy is our *personhood*, the
extraordinary mix of traits and talents
and experience that make up the *finger-
print of our souls*. This power belongs to us
and only us. Although there is a boun-
tiful supply of power for each of us, it
is, nonetheless, a precious thing. It ought
not be wasted. It must never be abused,
else it will come back to destroy us. It
can never be *abdicated or denied*, else we
will have lost *our very selves* in the process."
(Italics mine.) (Used by permission of the
author.)

The same can be said when, at eight years old, this
power was *stolen* from me. I did not *abdicate* or *deny*
it. I never had that chance. My abuser extinguished
the healthy process by which I might have *discov-*

ered my power and my legitimate claim to my self. Had I discovered it in time, I might have used it to tell the truth and expose him. But in my interactions with him, and with others around me, I had become convinced that I was power*less*. I have lived all these years believing that power belonged to everyone who laid claim to it. The rector, bishops, seminary deans, college presidents, parish wardens, even the collective idea of "the congregation," all were repositories of power. That I had endowed others with the power I perceived they had in my life came as a surprise to me.

Books kept coming. One day I found a box from Amazon at my door, sent by my brother. In it were two books by William Ury, the cofounder of Harvard's Program on Negotiation. The first was *Getting Past No*, published in 1993. The second, written fourteen years later, was titled *The Power of a Positive No*, published in 2007. Both books deal with the times in our lives when it is important for us to have the courage, the wit, and the finesse to say "NO," when to do otherwise would do us or someone else harm.

I noted the excellent advice in the first book, but I was greatly helped when I read the second. There, Ury uses a very helpful analogy. He asks us to imagine a tree with its roots, its trunk, and its crown (foliage and fruit). The roots represent the deep and desirable principles from which we derive our values, our overall "YES." From this reservoir, we formulate the "NO" that may be required to serve our positive goal. By rooting our "NO" there, we have a firmer resolve. That "NO" is the trunk of the tree. When our "NO" is successfully delivered, we will, hopefully, arrive at a "YES" that bears fruit for all who are involved. He writes:

> Perhaps the single biggest mistake we make when we say No is to *start* from No. We derive our No from what we are *against*—the other's demand or behavior. A Positive No calls on us to do the exact opposite and base our No on what we are *for.* Instead of starting from No, start from Yes. Root your No in a deeper Yes—a Yes to your core interests and to what truly matters . . .

> According to the sages of ancient India, there are three fundamental processes at work in the universe: creation, preservation, and transformation. Saying No is essential to all three processes. If you can learn how to say No skillfully and wisely,

you can *create* what you want, *protect* what you value, and *change* what doesn't work. These are the three gifts of a Positive No.*

I did not believe I had the power to say, "No" when I was eight, or ten, or even thirteen. Furthermore, I had no idea what my "Yes" might look like until I met the beautiful girl in the band and discovered the new possibilities of my own sexuality. My body and my power were not the rector's to possess. I was able to refuse his desire for me because I desired someone else with whom I could have a *reciprocal* romance, my "Yes." That much had changed. What had *not* changed were the other ramifications of my learned helplessness. I never gained the footing from which I could say "No" to his appeals to be restored to Holy Orders when I had the opportunities to do so. The admonition that I was never to tell had taken deep root. I was afraid to tell when I was eight, and I was afraid to tell when I was fifty.

---

*William Ury, *The Power of a Positive No—How to Say No and Still Get to Yes,* (New York: Bantam Dell, 2007). Available from Amazon.com **ISBN-13:** 978-0553384260 (used by permission)

Chapter Six

Convergence 2008 – 2012

J'accuse

The combination of connecting with my child through the teddy bear, the unqualified acceptance of "little Carl" by an understanding congregation, Gerry Spence's wisdom, and the attractive theory of Ury's books converged. One wintry January afternoon, having finished reading the second book, I reread my copious notes. I stood up, walked to my desk, picked up the teddy bear, and said out loud to "Little Carl" and my dog, Cobie, "It's time to say no." I had connected with something solid deep within myself.

I did not give it a second thought. I picked up my phone and called my former parishioner and friend, a well-known personal injury lawyer. I called him at his home. No one answered, so I spoke to his machine, "I want to talk to you about bringing a case against the man who sexually abused me when I was a child," I said. "Give me a call back." There! I had said it out loud to somebody who could help me formulate my No. But no one called me back. I tried again. Still, no call. My resolve did not abate.

This was something I was now determined to do. Finally, I called another gifted and astute personal injury lawyer who I had met when I was in court for a case he was trying. I had met him briefly when the court adjourned. It was a long shot. He barely knew me, but I *did* mention my connection when I called. While his secretary was discussing it with me, he picked up the phone and said, "I'll talk with him." She hung up, and for twenty minutes this man discussed my case with compassion and empathy. "This happened sixty years ago," I said.

"Is the man still alive?" he asked.

"Yes."

"Then I don't care how long ago it happened, maybe we can make it clear that no matter how long you get away with it, this sort of thing will come back to bite you." Here was an example to justify the very important step that many states have taken, to waive the statute of limitations in cases of child sexual abuse. As my story demonstrates, it can be a lifetime of struggle before the abused person can find the strength to take action. "I'll take the case," he said. "Let's meet and discuss the details; meanwhile, write me the story."

Two days before the meeting, I took the teddy bear and placed him with his head and hands looking over my computer screen. His beady little eyes watched as I began the narrative, which became the outline for this book. From that, my lawyer framed the formal complaint, filed it, and served it on my abuser. The notice informing me that the complaint had been served included a physical description of the rector. This man, who had seemed to be larger than life and invincible to me, whose threats had kept me in fear for a lifetime, was seven inches shorter than I. At ninety-five he had shrunk, literally and figuratively. He was a little man. Already, I was beginning to see him in a different light.

For the Plaintiff

Now other feelings were being stirred up. Fear clothed itself in new apparel. I began to have visions and dreams of being killed by a truck or maimed in a car crash. I knew this was irrational, but I could not shake it. I had mustered the strength to confront *him*, but in doing so, I had unleashed the fear of harm to *myself*. What if he decided to countersue me? What if I lost this case and was ordered to pay costs? I called my attorney and with a shaky voice shared these threatening thoughts. He assured me that these things were very unlikely. Next stop, Michael. "You think that the whole universe is going to contrive to prepare a big truck to arrive at the place in front of the curb just as you step out and pick you off all because of what?" he asked. I thought immediately, "If you ever tell, something terrible will happen to you—and me." The rector's voice again. We worked it out, the best way to deal with this persistent mantra was to face it squarely, once and for all. I would proceed with the suit.

Over the years, my brother had spent many hours helping me with memories. Indeed, he also had a powerful memory that had disturbed him since his own childhood. Eventually, he shared with me that he had also had a bewildering episode with the rector. I asked his permission to tell my attorney. When the attorney heard it, he immediately asked my brother if he would be willing to testify to the incident in a court of law. Since my brother struggles with a serious spinal disease that left him disabled by severe chronic pain, it was decided that his testimony should be videotaped for later use in the event that a court trial might ensue. The rector's counsel from a well-known local law firm would take part in the examination.

On a very hot summer day, I picked up my brother at his home and drove him to my attorney's office. As we entered, my attorney and his associate took us aside. They explained that there had been a change. While the local counsel would be present, an additional attorney was flying up from the city where the rector resided. She would be directing the questions. As a pediatrician, my brother had appeared in court cases involving abuse of children who he had treated in his practice. Therefore, he was accustomed to the procedure.

Soon the room was converted into something between a courtroom and a television studio. A videographer arrived and unpacked his camera, microphones, and other paraphernalia. Next, a woman arrived. She carried a large leather case from which she set up a small table with a steno-type machine, located next to the chair in which my brother would be seated. When the counsel for the defense arrived, she opened her briefcase, took out several files, and laid them out on the table. I was seated at the opposite end of the table behind the cameraman. I was most definitely not to appear on camera. When all had taken their places, my attorney took a moment to introduce each person present, ascertained if everyone was ready, and nodded to the cameraman. The stenotypist, who was also a notary public, asked my brother to raise his right hand and swore him in. I could tell that he was in a lot of pain. How strange, I thought, that while I was the plaintiff, it had fallen to *him* to be the one appearing for examination under oath. It was he who was bearing the most stressful part of the process so far.

My attorney began the questioning. "State your name . . . Relationship to the plaintiff . . . Since you have been disabled, how have you supported yourself? . . . Has there been any agreement with your brother to share any award that might result from this case? . . . Since you struggle with chronic pain, are you taking medication to control the pain." (*This, undoubtedly, was to ascertain his ability to testify accurately.*) "If you do not take pain killers, how do you live with your pain?" No one who has *not* suffered from unyielding, constant pain that one knows will never go away can comprehend what it is like. My brother knew this was not the place for a long explanation. Having read the dozens of poems he had written through his thirty years of suffering, I knew the enormity of what he left unsaid. His answer was simple, "I have had to make peace with my pain!" My attorney continued:

(*excerpts from the official transcript*)

"Dr. Russell, were you religious as a child?"

"I—I was brought up in the Congregational Church, and my mother and my father were religious, so I went to church. And then, I'm not sure which age I was, twelve or thereabouts, they joined the Episcopal Church."

"In the course of going to that Episcopal Church did you meet a Father Whipple?

"Yes. He was the rector there."

"Did your father have any relationship that you could observe with Father Whipple?"

"As I look back on it, yes, he had—Whipple was a—a hero to him. He worshiped Whipple. He—my father—was not very successful, obviously; and I think he saw this as a chance to step up."

"So, do you remember if you had an event with Father Whipple that you can remember vividly today?"

"Oh, yes I do."

"And would you please tell the ladies and gentlemen of the jury the event that you remember."

"Well, my brothers and I were very good acolytes. We were attentive to our duties; and—I had odd jobs at the church from time to time. And I remember two—do you mean me directly?"

"Yes."

"Yes. I have an outstanding memory, and that was I was doing something on the front steps to— going upstairs from his lower level (in the rectory). And I have the feeling that I was polishing a railing but that's—but anyway, as I got to the top step, whatever the circumstance was, I stood up to the top step. And the door to my left flew open and out pranced—I would say pranced Father Whipple. His hair was wet and he was wrapped in a towel. And—and I was on the top step, so I was watching him run by. And as he came to me, he— he was holding his towel—he had a towel. He was holding the towel with his right hand. He let go of the towel. The towel fortunately stayed in place. But with both hands he took my head and held it as he kissed me rather vigorously on the lips with his lips, which was very shocking to me. I mean, I didn't know what to make of that. And then he kept on to the right and went into his bedroom and shut the door."

My attorney went on to another question, but my brother interrupted.

"I have a couple of other memories that I should . . ."

"Yes?"

"They—they were—he and I never mentioned *that* episode. However, within a week or so he (the rector) called me up on a Saturday afternoon and asked me if I would go to the movies with him. And—I was naïve, but I wasn't that naïve—and I refused. Then the next week he called, and I wouldn't answer the phone. So my father talked to him. And my father said to me off to the side, 'Father Whipple wants to know if you will go to the movies with him.' I said, 'No, I won't.' And my father was obviously not happy with that response. And when he got off the phone, he said, 'Gee, you know, he—he's a lonely guy. He is a priest here. He doesn't have anything to do on Saturday. He is being nice. He is asking you out to the movies.' And I said, 'Well, I'm sorry. I don't want to go.' And that went on for about three weeks. Then it stopped."

"Dr. Russell, did there come a time when Father Whipple left Maine?

"Yes."

"And was the circumstance around which Father Whipple left Maine a matter of some discussion in your family?"

"Yes."

"Tell us."

"Well, I was—I was in medical school. This is to the best of my recollection. And I think we had one telephone on the floor of the dorm, and somebody came and called me and said, they want you on the phone. It was my father, and my father was obviously extremely upset. He was crying and sobbing and told me, 'They've arrested Father Whipple.' And I said, 'What do you mean?' He said, 'Well, they found out that he was providing booze to some East End teenagers who the police picked up; and they asked them where they got the booze, and they told them Father Whipple. And they went there, and I don't know how this all came down; but they took him—took him away.'"

"When that happened, did you tell your father that Father Whipple had kissed you on your lips?"

"No, no. I just told him—I told my father I was not surprised. And my father didn't seem to understand why I wasn't as upset as he was, but I was not upset at all."

"Now you told us earlier that you had a conversation in 1992 with your brother."

"Right."

"And was he a priest at that time?"

"Yes, he was."

"And did he tell you about his experience with Father Whipple?"

"Yes."

"What did he tell you?"

"It was the first time. I never knew anything about it before. Well, he told me that—he was the rector in Fitchburg, Massachusetts (at the time). I don't remember the name of the church. And anyway, he was standing at his sink. He was preparing or cleaning up from a meal and listening to public radio, and they were discussing child predators. And he burst out crying and . . ."

My brother's voice broke. "Excuse me . . ."

I saw a wave of remorse disfigure my brother's face. His whole countenance expressed grief. He lost his voice and began to weep. As I looked at him, I felt very, very sad that my case was causing him so much physical and emotional pain. He did not deserve this. He was struggling with the idea that if he had behaved differently, I would have been protected. I was overcome with feelings of gratitude for this brother who had done so much for me all my life, who was willing to go through such pain to corroborate my own memories. I had not known that, like me, he had carried a burden of shame, even though he had never been a willing participant in anything. I also began to cry. The room became silent, save for the sounds of our distress. My attorney spoke:

"Doctor, are you OK? If you need to take a break . . ."

"No."

"You want to get through this?"

My brother tried to regain his composure.

"It will take me a second."

"OK, sure. I know how hard this is."

Struggling to hold back his tears, my brother tried again.

"What's bothering me is that . . ." He began to cry again.

"Doctor?"

"You may want to wait a minute," my brother choked.

"OK. Let's go off camera for a minute."

The camera stopped. Someone offered us coffee. The tone of the room relaxed for a brief interval. Then the cameraman was instructed to begin again.

"Doctor, we took a short break. Do you want to go ahead now?"

"Yes."

"I think you were telling us *(my brother began to cry again)*—what is—what is it that is making you cry, what memory?"

"The memory is that I didn't do anything. I never did anything to protect him. Hold it a second—"

His voice faltered again. There was a pause.

"I should have known. I knew what kind of guy he was because I used to work in his gardens. He and his friends used to come out on the back deck. They were both priests, and I knew them. But they used to, you know, cavort around and touch each other inappropriately. I don't think that—I don't know how—they hugged each other. But I should have known; and I never—it never occurred to me—I don't think, in my own defense, I knew what predators were at that age—But then Carl told me what he had been through, that's when I felt — I told him Whipple had kissed me, which is no way near what he did to you, but it always bothered me."

The questioning continued until my attorney had finished. He then turned the questioning over to the defendant's counsel for cross-examination. After a number of questions about his illness, medication, his income, and asking whether, perhaps, he and I were in collusion to share any settlement, she proceeded.

"Did you start doing work at—around the church shortly after you joined the church?"

"A couple of years."

"A couple of years."

"I was an acolyte early on. And as far as I remember, you know, Carl and I were the only acolytes. There might have been others."

"There were other altar boys?"

"As I remember, we were it for a long time. There were—there were some others, as a matter of fact, later on because I noticed one of my best friends in jr. high school was going to church; and he became an acolyte, too. And there was another— another fellow who did; but they both quit being acolytes. I remember those because I remember them disappearing—you know, quitting."

"You remember what?"

"That they stopped being acolytes, which I could never figure out why they just suddenly disappeared; but now I have my opinions as to why they might have."

"When your father told you that Rev. Whipple had been arrested, why didn't you tell him what your suspicions were about Rev. Whipple?"

"I didn't dare to—the same reason I didn't when he first kissed me. I thought—I—I didn't know what was going on for a while after that, and I don't even know where I went after that. I did not go home and tell anybody. I know that because I never told anybody. I think I was afraid to because I—maybe two reasons—and this is maybe in retrospect—that I wouldn't be believed; and the second was that—well, as part of that actually, is that in the parish it would cause too much destructive . . ." My brother never finished his sentence. The rector's attorney continued:

"After Rev. Whipple was arrested—you were told this when you were in medical school—did you ask Carl if Rev. Whipple had ever touched him inappropriately?"

"I don't believe so. I didn't know then. I didn't ask him—"

"And when—"

"—which, again, doesn't help my guilt."

"When your brother told you what had happened to him, did you tell him he should sue his abuser?"

"No."

"Did you encourage him at any other time to sue him?"

"Yes, I did."

"When did you first encourage him to sue?"

"Well, after years of talking to him on the phone with him obviously not getting any better as far as his fear of him and the guilt and all of that, I said, you know, the way—probably, the only way to face him is in court. The only way you can become unafraid of him may be to sue him."

"Do you have any understanding why your brother chose now, when this man is ninety-five years old, to sue?"

"Well, I know his response to me over a few years of telling him he ought to was that he couldn't. He was too afraid."

After three brutal hours, the session was ended. The briefcases were rearranged, the microphones were collected, the camera disassembled, wires rewound. The stenotypist dismantled her machine and stowed it in its carrying case. But the feelings that had been unleashed in my brother and me were not so easily dispatched. People began to mumble to one another, but no one spoke to *us*. With barely a word of farewell, everyone disappeared. Bearing the pain, which plagued him daily, my brother carried an invisible burden of sadness and fatigue to the elevator. My attorney and his associate came to stand with us. They thanked my brother for doing such a great job and assured him that his testimony would be very helpful, shook hands, and returned to their office. We pushed the "G" button, rode down the five landings, and silently walked out into the sultry sunlight. "Thank you," I said. The words could barely carry the freight of my lifelong gratitude.

As we drove to his house, he said, "You have no idea what it means to me to have had this chance to tell the truth to someone. I had never told a soul about that incident, not even my wife. You have done me a favor. Now I can let it go."

The Gorilla in the Room

I had been warned that the process might be slow and that it could very well be a rough road. Months passed with little or no word. Then I received a copy of the defendant's countercomplaint. It argued that I had purposely waited until the defendant had reached an old age when he was defenseless and unable to secure witnesses for his own defense. As might be expected, it presented as damaging a picture of me as possible. The idea was to discredit me as a legitimate litigant. I wanted to shout, "What about the decades I have spent getting up the courage to do anything, trying to deal with the consequences of what he did to me? What did he care when *I* was weak and defenseless and unable to summon the help that would have put a stop to all of this?" I called my lawyer and registered my complaint. He patiently and calmly assured me that this was an expected response, legal boilerplate, he called it. "You relax," he said, "and leave the driving to us."

These legal documents, which represented my "No!" and made the whole thing a matter of public record, stirred feelings in me that I could not explain. The first was that I began to grieve for something I could not identify. Why was I feeling such sadness? I reported these feelings to Michael and we began to deal with the surprising reality that the finality of the documentation was pronouncing a death warrant to the fantasies I had held from that time to this that a special relationship might have existed. In my mind, I knew it never had been so, but somewhere else I discovered the remains of a hope that never could have been realized. For many, many years I had thought in some deep recess of my soul that when he died, I would receive notice that he had remembered me in his will with a note telling me how sorry he was for the things that he had done. I still wanted him to be the good person underneath it all, that I had been convinced to believe in by the people around me. Now, by my own hand, I had shattered that self-deception. My grief was rooted in moving from that childlike hopefulness to the grown-up truth that the rector had been a selfish abuser and not the loving adult I thought he was. It is hard to grow up.

The second was my deep feelings of sorrow for

him. Maybe the countercomplaint was correct. How *could* I be doing this to an old, ailing man? Perhaps the news of this complaint would cause him to have a heart attack. I was hurting him, the man we were all supposed to love. I envisioned him crying when he read that little Carl Russell was retaliating like this. I literally began to seek him out, this man whom I had feared for so long. I searched the Internet and found a picture of him. He was in a wheelchair. He was on dialysis. How could I be doing this? I began to castigate myself. I was so puzzled by this response that I shared it with my brother. Through his medical training, he was familiar with the literature on this. He sent me an e-mail; "Look up the Stockholm Syndrome." In an Internet article by Joseph M. Carver PhD, he explains this strange phenomenon, which comes as an inexplicable surprise to those who experience it.

> On August 23rd, 1973, two machine-gun-carrying criminals entered a bank in Stockholm, Sweden. Blasting their guns, one prison escapee named Jan-Erik Olsson announced to the terrified bank employees, "The party has just begun!" The two bank robbers held four hostages, three women and one man, for the next 131 hours. The hostages were strapped

with dynamite and held in a bank vault until finally rescued on August 28. After their rescue, the hostages exhibited a shocking attitude considering they were threatened, abused, and feared for their lives for over five days. In their media interviews, it was clear that they supported their captors and actually feared law enforcement personnel who came to their rescue. The hostages had begun to feel the captors were actually protecting them from the police. One woman later became engaged to one of the criminals and another developed a legal defense fund to aid in their criminal defense fees. Clearly, the hostages had "bonded" emotionally with their captors. While the psychological condition in hostage situations became known as "Stockholm Syndrome" due to the publicity, the emotional "bonding" with captors was a familiar story in psychology. It had been recognized many years before and was found in studies of other hostage, prisoner, or abusive situations such as: abused children, battered/abused women, prisoners of war, cult members, incest victims, criminal hostage situations, concentration camps, prisoners, controlling/intimidating relationships. In the final analysis, emotionally bonding with an abuser is actually a strategy for survival for victims of abuse and intimidation. The "Stockholm Syndrome" reaction in hostage and/or abuse situations is so well recognized at this time that police hostage negotiators no longer view it as unusual.

The article helped to explain a moment in Michael's office on the day he had placed the teddy bear on my knee. I had told "little Carl" that I was sorry for not protecting him. Having said that, Michael said, "Tell him that the man who did this to you was evil." My emotions came to a dead stop. I could not say those words. To me "evil" meant depraved, possessing no redeeming value, absolutely void of any good whatsoever. How could he be evil? He was my priest! I managed to say, "The man who did this to you was sick."

"Really?" Michael whispered.

I looked up and said, "Yes, he was a sick man."

As we unpacked this baggage, I began to see that as long as I could pronounce him a sick man, I could care for him, put on my "pastor" hat. I could excuse him and make allowances at the expense of the little guy sitting on my knee. I had said the right words when I promised to protect him, but even as I said them, I attenuated the enormity of what was done to us. It took several more tries with explanation and remonstrance before I finally mumbled, "*What he did was very evil.*" There, I had said that word, "evil." But I never could bring myself to say, "*He* is evil." And what I *did* say I said as softly as possible.

Michael said, "What are you feeling right now?"

"Well, I am actually pretty angry," I replied. I looked over at a big, black, stuffed gorilla sitting on the futon across from me. I never said anything out loud, but in my mind I shouted at the gorilla, "You evil son of a bitch! Look what you have done to us!" I would not be able to say it aloud until after our work on the Stockholm Syndrome was done.

All I Have to Do Is Dream . . .

The following Thursday I recorded an important dream. The italics inserted as I write it are the notes made by my wife as I interpreted the dream with my therapist.

Dream One

The Pope is visiting. His face is that of Christopher Plummer, the actor.

My wife immediately picked up that this is an impostor. My therapist helped me discover that this impostor has taken over my own Pope archetype.

A group of people is preparing to participate in the Liturgy that is to follow. We are all located in a "vesting room" (in the dream I know it is a sacristy, but I am unable to acknowledge that). I think we are at a cathedral of some sort.

The cathedral represents "my world" both inside and beyond the church in which I have spent my whole life.

One man in the room is the person who gets to appoint the Archbishop of Canterbury and the Pope. He is called "The Judge."

All of these figures are "interior," not external. The Judge is a part of my own personhood [which I have always said was what was robbed by my abuser]. I am the Judge who gets to decide who is Archbishop of Canterbury and who is Pope (these are the most powerful church figures in my world). This is the place that has been occupied by the rector in my life, and I am about to take authority as I sit in the Judge's chair. This is not about the courtroom that may or may not happen in the exterior world as part of my lawsuit.

The Judge begins questioning the Pope, saying, "What do you do all day? What good are you? Who do you think you are? You think you have power, but I tell you, you are powerless." The Pope (all of a sudden) is no longer in white robes.

As Judge, I have deposed him and called his right to have authority in my psyche into question.

His robes have turned red (the liturgical color for a martyr).

This is a fleeting reference to my struggle with the Stockholm Syndrome, feeling that I am hurting someone who I'm not supposed to hurt.

He begins crying and I am astonished.

I can't believe that the Judge—this part of myself — has the power to depose the Pope.

By my authority he IS powerless. He is lying on the floor. His robe has now turned purple, the liturgical color for penitence. His robes are now made of silk and he is weeping.

The dream is now giving me clues as to who the Pope is. The rector used to greet me at the rectory door in his silk dressing gown. He had played the part of the ecclesiastical authority, the one in control of my "self." I do not feel any

sadness about his weeping, just amazement that the Pope is
powerless and reduced to a weakling lying on the floor crying.

The group continues to vest. I am vesting in
an alb.

In church terms, this is the vestment worn for sacra-
mental acts (transformational acts) such as Holy Eucharist
[bread into body of Christ], Baptism [from death into life],
Marriage [no longer two but one].

Someone says, "You can't wear an alb. We are
at war."

The war referred to is the war within myself to retake
my own authority in my life—the warfare between the
impostor (signified by the fact that the Pope wears the face
of a well-known actor) and my own authentic Pope, myself.

The person continues, "You have to wear
chancel dress during war time."

Chancel dress denotes the vestments worn for services
that do not require ecclesiastical authority to perform. In
other words, until this interior warfare is settled and I have
taken back the authentic power of my own self, which has
been robbed in my childhood, I cannot act with authority.
This is a war that has gone on in me for a long time, what
I have always called my 'love-hate' relationship with the
church.

As I am changing vestments, I say to the Judge and the others, "I don't know about you, but even if I AM *and* Anglican, I want a strong Pope!"

My therapist picks up the capital "I AM" and the inadvertent use of "and" instead of "an" following it. The "I AM" then becomes a statement of regained power. ("I Am" is the name God gives Moses when Moses asks, "Who shall I say is sending me?") In other words, if the Pope is the authentic Pope in me, I want that Pope to be strong—in charge, worthy of being followed by the rest of my psyche.

The Pope then seems to have recovered his power, but he no longer carries the face of the actor.

Note that this Pope no longer is played by an actor. I am not clear what his face looks like, but it is not the face of an actor. My therapist says this face will be revealed. As I write this, I suspect that it is my own *face.*

The Pope is now dressed in white again. I look at him and say, "I always was a good acolyte."

If I have appointed the authentic Pope to his rightful place in my psyche, then I can be a good acolyte to that. In other words, it's appropriate, taking my signals from the authentic power in myself, to trust that and attend to it [which is what an acolyte does] and carry out with strength the things my rightful Pope declares (namely, the NO I am determined to act upon in my litigation). End of dream.

Dream Two

Ten days later, as if to punctuate this insight, I had another dream. I am facing the rector eye to eye. I am angry and ceremonially removing his rabat. The rabat is an article of clergy attire—a bib-like vest with a clerical collar attached that traces its origins to the waistcoat in English dress. Another name for this article is a "frock."

I am literally defrocking him. This dream seems to be rooted in my anger at the bishop, the diocese, and the Standing Committee, who reinstated the rector to active priesthood, and anger at myself for not intervening when I had the opportunity.

Frock You!

Unbeknownst to me, when he *had* been defrocked, the rector sent his set of rabats (his frocks) and his tippet (a scarf worn with a cassock and surplice for chancel dress) to my mother with a note instructing her to see that they were given to me on the occasion of my ordination. She complied with his wishes, and on my Ordination Day, she gave them to me, neatly arranged in an L.L. Bean box. In this insidious way, he inserted himself into this special day. He was not a welcome guest. I carried that box around in my bureau drawer for many years, though I never wore the things it contained. When

I inadvertently opened that drawer, I would feel inexplicable anger toward my mother, though she had no idea what they would mean to me.

I wore clerical dress for most of my career until the time of the shocking breakthrough at the kitchen sink. As the memories became more vivid, I could no longer stand to be identified in that way. I finally took the rabats out of the drawer and with pleasure and a sense of relief, I took them to the dump and chucked them into the garbage. From then on I never took a clerical shirt out of the drawer, and my own collars remained in their storage case on my dresser. It was not that I had made a conscious decision not to use them. I just did not use them. Instead I wore dress shirts and ties. Somehow, it set me free. The congregation had not been used to this, and there were people who thought it was their privilege to take me to task for it. I simply told them that I now preferred plain dress.

This worked until I became rector of a very large and prominent parish in another diocese. The people there had been used to clerical dress. While most had no issue at all with my preference, someone apparently felt it was their duty to inform the bishop that I was not wearing traditional attire and that "lots of people were upset by it." As is so common in the church, no one ever spoke to me directly to ask for my reasons. Soon, I had a call from the bishop asking me to meet with him in his office. When we were seated, he raised the question by saying, "Carl, someone has called to complain that you are not wearing a clerical collar. Clergy in this diocese wear clerical collars." I knew that there was no such rule in the church. In most dioceses it is a matter of choice.

I thought to myself, "There must be really serious issues in the church that we could be talking about, but this is surely not one of them." I liked this bishop very much. He was a fine man and his life story was inspiring. He was also the bishop under whom my wife was bound toward her own ordination. I respected him, and I trusted him enough to tell him the whole truth of why I could not bring myself to dress up in the clothes that my abuser had taken such delight and pride in. As I told him, I lost my composure and asked for his understanding. To his great credit, he immediately moved from a matter of quasi-discipline to a most empathetic and understanding attitude. He told me how very sorry he was to hear of the pain I was in and the ways in which it inhibited so many aspects of my life. This was the first time I had ever mentioned my abuse to a bishop. He represented the church well, with love and concern for me. It was an important component of the many things that had made it possible for me to take action against my abuser.

Triumph!

As the leaves were falling from the maple trees in my back yard, I became anxious that no word had been heard from "the defendant." I had called my attorney several times to ask if we were to go to court or not. He explained that the other side had until the twenty-fifth of the month to respond to our complaint. Three more weeks. Waiting was the hardest part. The tension I felt told me that the outcome of this action was very important to the recovery of my integrity. By the "NO" I had declared in my formal complaint, I was to discover whether I was right or wrong in my conclusion as a child that I would never be believed. Secretly, I hoped for a trial by jury. What would it mean to hear a jury of common folk declare that what I was remembering was true, that finally there would be a verdict.

On the twenty-fifth of the month, my lawyer called. "Carl, get ready. They want to talk today. We are to have a conference call at two o'clock p.m. I will call you as soon as I know anything.

Will you be around this afternoon?" I assured him that, whatever else I might have had planned, I would be at my phone whenever he called. At 2:20 p.m. my phone rang. "Carl, are you sitting down?"

"I will be in a second," I answered.

"They don't want this to go to court," he went on. "They want to settle. It is much more than we would have thought possible in a tort this old!"

When I heard the amount I realized that this was as close to an apology as I would ever get. I would never hear the answer of a jury, but this concession was verdict enough. My attorney went on, "We strongly recommend that you settle. You would be wise to decide and answer promptly." There was one catch. They wanted to gag me. The settlement called for me to agree that I would never divulge the story. Once again, I was faced with the injunction "No Telling Aloud!" This time it would be written in stone, legally binding. I asked for time to discuss it with my wife. We were of one mind that such an agreement would only intensify my frustration and sense of powerlessness. We discussed the gag order with my attorney, and he renegotiated the settlement. Rather than hold out for more money, we would agree to silence while my abuser was alive, but I would be free to tell my story upon his death. It would be well worth whatever we took as a monetary loss, and it made the writing of this book possible. With that crucial stipulation, I accepted. I was overjoyed. I had put to rest the fantasy that somehow *he* would voluntarily make restitution one day, that he would remember me in his will. Instead, *I* took the action that set a price on what he had done and claimed a value for myself.

Several days later, I went to the attorney's office to finalize the settlement. There were papers to be signed, explanations to be made, discussion of terms. Finally, I was presented the official document. At the bottom of the final page were the lines awaiting the signatures of the two parties. There, before my eyes, was the familiar signature from so many years ago in the same hand that had written, "I will always be your Father." He had been compelled to read the complaint (my NO), acknowledge it, and affix his signature to the consequence of what he had done, which was the settlement. A crucial transfer was taking place here and now, but it was not about the transfer of funds. It was the transfer of shame. By his signature, he took on the shame of the things that had happened between us. Though he might never admit it, I had received a sacramental apology. By affixing *my own* signature, I would also sign away the burden that had beset me all my life. Holding the teddy bear on the table beside me, aligned in the viewfinder of my wife's iPhone, I picked up the pen and signed my name.

Now What?

I never thought it would be about money. I assumed I should be above that, but the fact is that there *is* something to having a value pronounced on the worth of my childhood. At the very least, it was about money and, though no amount of money can repay the debt, in our culture money is able to stand symbolically for other things. In a tangible way this placed a value on the intangible and irretrievable childhood he had stolen from me. Yet my mind would not allow me to fully "receive" the settlement. I struggled with the notion that somehow, taking this money turned the whole sordid business into some sort of prostitution. I was getting *paid* for something awful I had done. This took me by surprise, and it didn't go away.

On the day I received the settlement check I was overjoyed, but as I actually had to contend with it, it made me very uncomfortable. I felt that I had come by it through devious means, that somehow it was not deserved. It still connected me to the trauma I had experienced. My wife helped me see other possibilities. She had substantial medical needs. We built an addition on our house. We used some for travel we had always hoped to enjoy. We used a lot of it to help other people make it through the economic meltdown. I could do *that,* but I could not spend any of it on myself, not even to buy a new watch. Now all the money is gone, and I feel a sense of relief. It sounds crazy, but that is how it is. Remember the invisible dog?

Moment of Silence

I was at the Gulf Coast condominium of dear friends to work on the manuscript of this book when my wife handed me the phone. "It is your brother," she said. I took the phone and said hello. After a brief silence, he said, "I am calling to let you know that the rector is dead." Silence. My mind was in free fall, unfettered, on an excursion of its own. Time stopped. I was transported to the soft, shaded place under a blossoming cherry tree on the mall in Washington, DC, just at the foot of the steps of the Lincoln Memorial. August of 1963. Two hundred fifty thousand of us gathered from all over the country in solidarity with the African Americans who were struggling for the passage of the Civil Rights Act. The Rev. Dr. Martin Luther King, Jr. was one hundred feet from where I was lying under a cherry tree at this moment of history in which we shared. It is one of those moments that ought to be remembered with passion and drama, but we had ridden all night on a bus without sleep. His voice was mellifluous and, as he spoke, it was like listening to a beautiful song. "I have a dream today . . . I have a dream . . ." I had lost track of the words. The melody of his voice had lulled me into a solitary peace. I heard those final words, but the power of that moment was lost in my semi-conscious fatigue. They took cover in my memory for another time. The time had come. As all of this happened in a flash of synapses firing at will; my brother heard only the silence. "Are you still there?" he asked. The thunderous cheering and applause were echoing all around me. "Free at last," I heard. "Free at last. Thank God Almighty, free at last." My brother's voice startled me. "Yes," I said, "I'm here."

Reading the Obituaries

A week after the rector died, I received an e-mail with a web address. I followed it to the page where I found two obituaries. The first surprised me. There, as it appeared in the New York Times, was the Bachrach photo that had its place on the gate leg table in my childhood. The accompanying article was the usual recounting of the facts of the rector's life. The second was more than a surprise; it was a shock, someone I barely knew. This was his self-authored obituary, which he had instructed to be read at his funeral service. It was the history of his life, garnished as he wished it to be remembered—colorful, impressive. Not surprisingly, as I read it, I was meeting someone entirely different from the person who had been my unwelcome hidden companion for all these years. It was like a match setting fire to the kindling of my resentments. From his sudden disappearance on that August day so long ago to the time of his death, fifty-five years had passed. He had gotten to write his version of the life to which he had been set free by the bishop, the county attorney, the diocesan chancellor, the senior warden, my father, and, yes, by *me*.

Then I read the letters of condolence from people who loved him, respected him, telling of the ways in which he had touched their lives. But they did not know what I knew. And what we don't know can't spoil our heartfelt, closely held opinions about the person we *think* we know. This began a struggle in me. What could I say to this other picture portrayed by him and so many others? Every testimony was to his credit. This felt like it felt when I was little, people all around me saying how wonderful he was. What about the rest of the story, the hidden secrets I carried all my life?

The obituaries are a matter of record, one in the memories of those who were present to hear his own version read aloud, the other in the archives of the New York Times. His version wins. Until now!

We Interrupt This Program . . .

It is Friday night, June 22, 2012. It is 9:53 p.m. The show I am watching on MSNBC has been interrupted. Sandusky is guilty! Jerry Sandusky, the assistant coach at Penn State, was tried in a court of law for the same things that I had experienced for six years; guilty on forty-five out of forty-eight counts of sexually abusing, exploiting, using young boys in the showers, in his basement, and who knows where else. Someone saw, and someone had the courage to tell it aloud to someone else. When he did, he was attacked for not intervening in what he saw. Mike McQueary told Joe Paterno, the legendary coach of the Penn State team, and the story stalled there. Because he told, McQueary became a victim of hateful slurs and e-mails. That is the price he paid for finally exposing the scandal. It went up the chain of command, but everybody who *could* postpone it *did* postpone it—for *nine* years! Who wants to spoil the reputation of a Jerry Sandusky? Who wants to implicate an institution as famous as Penn State? Who cares enough to blow the lid off years of young people molested, threatened, frightened, confused, and sometimes ruined? Think of the consequences, the waves of disruption. This sounds painfully familiar to me, the same questions that were asked in the bishop's office fifty-four years ago.

My emotions begin to catch up with me. Every muscle is taut with anxiety. Or anger? Or outrage? The defense attorney, Joe Amendola, is speaking to the crowd gathered at the courtroom steps. They jeer whenever he says anything in Sandusky's defense. He announces that the sentence will likely be sixty years. A cheer erupts. Sandusky will most likely die in prison. "He got what he deserves," they say. "You're damned right!" I say. What a difference a half century makes! Zero tolerance, prosecutors who actually prosecute, lancing the boil, and getting the entire stench open to the air and the light, the very things that should have happened to my abuser. I am relieved that it is so.

But there are other emotions swirling in my head and my heart as if they have been thrown together in a smoothie-bar blender. I want to be *in* the crowd, but I don't particularly want to be *like* the crowd. "Hang him!" someone yells. As they lead him immediately from the court to the jail cell, the anchor explains, "He will need protection." Protection from the outrage of the people, not just the families of the children involved, but the general population who find this repulsive. "Scum bag!" I hear, as Amendola tries again to speak.

I wonder if there would have been an outcry like this when I was little? Not likely, I think. My abuser? Well, he got off scot-free! The Powers That Be, including the prosecutor, contrived to make it all go away. How many counts was that? The two juveniles and me, that makes at least three. The thirty years Sandusky will spend in prison? My abuser spent them free as a bird—another degree, a better job, a life of ease at his island escape, building his fortune and a new reputation. Those feelings are racing around in that blender, but there is something else! Something is emerging as I watch, and my emotions move along to the thing that is most important of all. As sad as I am for my inner child, and as angry as I am that my abuser went on unscathed, I am feeling so much joy for the children who finally got truth on their side, who were finally free to speak up, to tell their stories aloud to someone! They got to hear a jury pronounce a verdict on their behalf. And not just them. There are so many others who have been left alone in silence. It's about them, not him. It's about them, and it's about me. I want to be in the crowd, but I want to shout "Hooray! for the kids and for their future. Hooray for *us*!" I want to find the team of prosecutors who pored over the evidence and put this case together, the jury who took the time to do the case justice, literally. I want to say, "Thank-you! Thank-you for taking the charges seriously. Thank-you for deliberating carefully. Thank-you for pronouncing the verdict I have longed to hear for sixty years."

Here He Lies

During the years that had passed since the deaths of my father, my mother, and my oldest brother, I had not been able to bring myself to return to the churchyard cemetery behind the rectory. I had never made peace with it. There was too much to remember there. With the story told, I was ready to go there and visit their graves. It was a crisp October day. As I drove into the church campus, I passed the familiar sacristy, which now displayed a splendid new oak door with beautifully fashioned wrought iron hinges. I slowed to look more closely. The door was not the only change. There was the window that had been comprised of the bits and pieces of plain colored glass. The faux glass was gone and a fine genuine stained glass window was there in its place. A new memorial window had been given. The donor was none other than the rector himself. As I drove past I wondered, *What is being remembered in that window? I know what I am remembering.*

I reached the cemetery entrance and sat for a moment, looking around me at the rectory, the tower, the gardens. Then I left the car and walked down a beautifully manicured path toward my parents' plots at the back of the grove. On my way I passed the markers of many people I had known and admired as a young child of the parish family. It was peaceful there. A breeze stirred in the low hanging branches as I wandered about searching for the small, plain rock that marked my parents' graves. It had been taken from under the back porch of the house where I grew up, in which they had lived for sixty-two years, a simple rock that my mother had cherished. But I did not find the place. I decided to give it up and come back another day. Then, as I turned to make my way to my idling car, I spied a slender, gracefully tapered birdbath, carved from the familiar red-stone granite of the church. It was nestled in a quiet corner of the grove, nearly lost in the shadows of the afternoon light. I approached for a closer look. Kneeling on the soft, mossy ground, I read the message engraved in script from the broad top to its slender base:

CHARLES
EVERETT
WHIPPLE

PRIEST
AND
DOCTOR

As if nothing had happened at all.

AFTERWORD
(To You, If You Have Been Sexually Abused)

Victim/Victorious

For all these years I felt that I was a victim. The things I read reinforced the idea that I had been *victimized*. News about children all over the world being abused by their priests in the Roman Catholic Church repeated that word constantly. But as long as I thought of myself as a victim, I perpetuated the scenery of my childhood experience. Whenever I thought *victim*, he was the one in charge. However, for me, the greater damage was done over a lifetime by the secrecy to which I, myself, subscribed. It was not only my seducer, but also the whole culture within which the episodes took place that secured that silence. Much of the success of silence was achieved by fear and shame. Even a child experiences shame, though s/he may not have a word for it. It was not my cooperation in the sexual moments as much as my collaboration in the veil of secrecy that did the greatest harm in my life. For me, there was an important journey to be made from this secrecy in childhood to acknowledgment in adulthood. It was not an easy path. It required years of therapy, the understanding of my wife and children, the courage to name the demons that stalked me, and finally to take action. It is in this journey that we move from victim to victor.

Merriam-Webster defines victor as "one who defeats an enemy; the winner." More importantly, included in the root of the word is a Lithuanian derivative, "veikti," meaning "to take action." Victory is about action. Letting sleeping dogs lie is unlikely to bring peace to anyone who bears within him or herself the scars and refuse left there by selfish, driven, and sick adults. I tried that for years. We become victors by acting on the truth. There is no shame in that. Owning our truth is the very thing that sets us free. That is the beginning of new life, no matter how old we may be. Over the lintel of the main entrance to my youngest son's house is posted a wonderful sign, which reads:

It is never too late to have a happy childhood!

AUTHOR'S NOTE

The account of what transpired between the men in the bishop's office where the deal was struck is written from my father's detailed description as he sat at the table with my mother and me and in later conversations with the rest of the family.

My brother's testimony is taken verbatim from portions of the record of the proceedings.

What happened to me took place more than sixty years ago, 1944 to 1954. The story is not about the congregation, either then or now. It is about a culture of silence, a broken system, myself, one man, and the place he occupied—physically and figuratively. The parish inhabiting the campus today is a vibrant, healthy, and devoted company of good people.

I am eager to meet you who have taken the time to read this through to the end. Perhaps I can answer questions or gladly receive your comments. Of course, I would appreciate your review of the book. I can be reached by e-mail at:

notellingaloud@yahoo.com

SUGGESTED READING

In the Shadow of the Cross, Charles Bailey, Jr.
iUniverse, Inc. 2021 Pine Lake Road, Suite 100
Lincoln, NE 68512
ISBN 0-595-40578-9 Available at Amazon.com.
An excellent autobiography of severe sexual abuse
at the hands of a Roman Catholic priest and helpful
guidelines for recovery. It describes many parallels
with my own experience.

Restoring the Soul of a Church, Editors: Nancy Myer
Hopkins and Mark Laaser
The Liturgical Press, Collegeville, Minnesota
56321
ISBN 0-8146-2333-6 Available from Amazon.com
This is a compendium of excellent articles dealing
with dysfunctional church systems and strategies
for dealing with the aftermath of clergy sexual
abuse. It explains the kind of care that has evolved
in the church since the time of my own abuse.

Silent No More, Aaron Fisher, Michael Gillum,
Dawn Daniels
Ballantine Books, Random House, Inc. NY
ISBN 978-0-345-54416-2 Available from Amazon.com

Jerry Sandusky's Victim # 1 speaks out and tells his story. Though I did not know him, Victim # 1 is one of the people I so much identified with on the night of Sandusky's conviction.

The Right Touch, Sandy Kleven, Jody Bergsma
Illumination Arts Publishing Co.
P.O. Box 1865, Bellevue, Washington 98009
ISBN 0-935699-10-4 Available from Amazon.com
A wonderful read-aloud book for parents to share with their children to teach them the
difference between appropriate and inappropriate "touching." Such books were not available to my parents when I was coping with these troubles.

When a Congregation Is Betrayed, Beth Ann Gaede, Ed.
The Alban Institute, Washington, DC
ISBN 1-56699-284-2 Available from Amazon.com
This book deals largely with adult victims of clergy abuse and addresses the larger issue of power imbalance and breach of fiduciary responsibility. It also describes the impact on congregations and describes specific protocols for helping congregations. Chapter 22, "Remembering the Victim," by Nancy Myer Hopkins, was of particular help to me.

CPSIA information can be obtained at www.ICGtesting.com
Printed in the USA
LVOW12s0715171113

361613LV00005B/565/P